Praise for *Spee[...]*

"David Kaye has been an outstanding UN Special Rapporteur on freedom of expression, and in this report he pungently distils his findings on one of the most important issues of our time."

—Timothy Garton Ash,
author of *Free Speech: Ten Principles for a Connected World*

"*Speech Police* is an essential primer for understanding the toughest global governance problem of our digital age. The future of human rights and democracy depends on whether the exercise of government and private power across globally networked digital platforms can be constrained and held accountable."

—Rebecca MacKinnon,
author of *Consent of the Networked*

"This is an important, timely, and provocative book on a hugely important topic. Everyone interested in free expression and social media should (and will) read it."

—Noah Feldman,
Felix Frankfurter Professor, Harvard Law School

"In this accessible, urgent volume, Kaye takes us on a whirlwind global tour of social media's sites of impact, from on-the-ground reports of activists in dangerous political climates to the candid conversations behind the closed doors of corporate boardrooms and the halls of government alike. A must-read for anyone invested in the issues this book touches: in other words, all of us."

—Sarah Roberts,
Assistant Professor of Information Studies, UCLA

"*Speech Police* doesn't merely surface the key questions surrounding platform governance and content moderation with flair and brevity—it also introduces us to the varied people and institutions asking and answering them."

—Jonathan Zittrain,
George Bemis professor of international law, Harvard University

COLUMBIA GLOBAL REPORTS
NEW YORK

Speech Police
The Global Struggle to Govern the Internet

David Kaye

Published by Columbia Global Reports
91 Claremont Avenue, Suite 515
New York, NY 10027
globalreports.columbia.edu
facebook.com/columbiaglobalreports
@columbiaGR

Library of Congress Control Number: 2019932096
ISBN: 978-0-9997454-8-9
E-book ISBN: 978-9997454-9-6

Book design by Strick&Williams
Map design by Jeffrey L. Ward
Author photograph by Ron Dassa
Creative Commons cover icons (left to right) all courtesy of The Noun Project: Talk
Bubble © diambergerak, ID; Ear Phones © Karen Tyler, GB; Microphone © John Caserta,
US; Volume by Krishna; Ear © Scott Lewis, US

Printed in the United States of America

The Net must offer a place for us, which means it must in a tangible sense "belong" to us. Anything else, at least with respect to democracy, is hypocrisy.

—Benjamin Barber,
"Which Technology and Which Democracy?" (1998)

United
States

CONTENTS

Introduction

Hossein Derakhshan went to prison with one internet and was released to another.

Derakhshan, known as the Iranian "blogfather" for his role in making Farsi blogging possible, helped invent Iranian blog culture; his technical insights gave Iranians the tools to use the popular Blogger platform by writing and reading Persian script. A widely read and at times controversial blogger and activist, Derakhshan had been critical of both the Iranian government and foreign threats to overthrow it, and he spent a considerable amount of time in self-imposed exile in Canada and Europe during a productive period of his blogging. During this period, he even visited Israel and wrote about it on his blog. In 2008, just two weeks after returning home to Tehran, the government arrested and then prosecuted Derakhshan for "spreading propaganda against the Islamic system," in addition to blasphemy and other criminal wrongdoing under the laws of the Islamic Republic. The prosecutor asked for Derakhshan's execution. He was found guilty, as anyone who knew anything about Iran's

criminal justice system expected, and sentenced to a cruel 19.5   11
years in jail.

Derakhshan was sent to Evin Prison, Iran's infamous detention center for political opponents, journalists foreign and domestic, unlucky visitors, and common criminals. He recalled the moment late in 2014 when he was released. Sipping tea with the dozen other men who shared his cell, he heard the announcement: "Dear fellow inmates, the bird of luck has once again sat on one fellow inmate's shoulders. Mr. Hossein Derakhshan, as of this moment, you are free."

Derakhshan has become a creative thinker about the culture of information and public debate online, with a perspective that owes something to his imprisonment. Like Rip Van Winkle, upon his release, he was able to reflect clearly on how the internet had changed. In 2008, Iran removed him from a world in which the internet was relatively decentralized, where individual bloggers were still able to influence media consumption. In 2014, it released him into the world of social media.

In blog culture, Derakhshan wrote, one's currency was the hyperlink, the way in which a writer and reader could choose to connect from one story to another. You might be reading one blog, be intrigued in the middle of it by a link to another blogger's ideas, then by a link to a news story, and so on, until suddenly you weren't sure how or why you got there. It was distracting but also a remarkable way to feed one's curiosity, a kind of random, limitless exploration of the world of ideas or entertainment or news or whatever you wanted. To be sure, it was moderated; blogs had (and still have) comment sections that could be more or less open to user input. Yet autonomy and expression were the overriding values, text was the medium,

12   and openness was its foundation. That web still exists, and it's
      what Derakhshan fights to save. But by the time he left Evin
      Prison, the audience had moved elsewhere. Instead of a web of
      blogs and news sites, he saw that social media had transformed
      the internet into something more like television, with its cen-
      tralization, sensationalism, insularity, and inward-looking
      approach. Lost was the horizontal and found was the vertical
      web, what journalist Alexis Madrigal called "nowness" and
      others referred to as "the Stream." As Derakhshan explained it:

> The Stream means you don't need to open so many websites
> anymore. You don't need numerous tabs. You don't even need
> a web browser. You open Twitter or Facebook on your smart-
> phone and dive deep in. The mountain has come to you. *Algo-
> rithms have picked everything for you.* According to what you or
> your friends have read or seen before, they predict what you
> might like to see. It feels great not to waste time in finding
> interesting things on so many websites.

While blogs survived, thrived, or failed in an ecosystem
of linking and comment threads, social media depended on
the chronologically new and on an emotional credentialing of
likes and hearts and retweets, which inevitably morphed into
the emojization of reactions. Autonomy and the thrill of ran-
domness gave way to timelines and news feeds driven by opaque
algorithms, "making us all much less powerful in relation to
governments and corporations," as Derakhshan observed.
Social media streamlined surveillance and monitoring, making
human behavior predictable and controllable, but Derakhshan
found "being controlled" was actually much "more frightening
than being merely watched."

A centralizing internet dominated by the corporate imperatives of advertising and data mining and the incentives of virality is, as Derakhshan and others have maintained, a much friendlier environment to "manufactured amplification," just as it is friendlier to censorship, hate speech, disinformation, and propaganda than the horizontal web of blogs and websites. Before the emergence of social media and monopolistic search, hateful propaganda would have had as good a chance of getting a foothold in American culture as a racist John Birch Society pamphlet in 1963—which is to say, it would have a following and provoke some discussion and hand-wringing, but a lack of enabling online amplification would not earn it the cultural coin that similar material today has permitted, such as radio host and conspiracy theorist Alex Jones's InfoWars website.

Derakhshan's insights bring to mind Lawrence Lessig's seminal work, *Code*. Lessig, a professor at Harvard, influenced a generation of students, technologists, and lawyers by positing that internet architecture is a form of law—that code is law. Architecture could protect freedom of expression and, as originally configured, limit the state's ability to constrain it:

> Relative anonymity, decentralized distribution, multiple points of access, no necessary tie to geography, no simple system to identify content, tools of encryption—all these features and consequences of the internet protocol make it difficult to control speech in cyberspace. The architecture of cyberspace is the real protector of speech there.

No single actor could be expected to police a horizontal web. This was the beauty of the internet at the time Derakhshan lost his connection to it. But then Lessig continues:

The first-generation internet might well have breached walls of control. But there is no reason to believe that architects of the second generation will do so, or not to expect a second generation to rebuild control. There is no reason to think, in other words, that this initial flash of freedom will not be short-lived.

Today's internet requires powerful, identifiable actors who police their own platforms and provide the keys for governments to police them as well. Danny O'Brien, the head of international advocacy at the Electronic Frontier Foundation, one of Silicon Valley's oldest and biggest digital rights advocacy groups, put it to me this way: "You *need* the companies to exist if you want to control speech."

The old internet was hard to police. As Bill Clinton famously said about China's hope to control the internet, "Good luck! That's sort of like trying to nail Jell-O to the wall." But the contemporary internet is nothing like Jell-O. It facilitates control by companies and governments: censorship and abuse, repression and disinformation. It allows for social media companies to regulate every piece of content—and it gives governments the targets for regulation and surveillance. The puzzle is how to deal with this threat: how to regulate it, in a way that protects fundamental human rights.

"Who is in charge?"

This was the question that Roberto Viola, the head of the European Commission's division responsible for communications network, content, and technology ("DG-CONNECT" in Euro-speak), wanted me to know was at the top of his mind. Meeting at his office on the outskirts of Brussels during the

summer of 2018, Viola walked me through the issues on his
plate, a menu of ills (and perceived ills) that people face on the
internet. But he started our conversation by noting that one
simple question must be answered in order to get internet regulation correct: *Who is in charge?*

Put another way, who polices speech online? Who ensures
the protection of individual rights on the internet? Who makes
the rules that govern online expression? Who enforces them?
Who adjudicates disputes concerning their enforcement? The
companies? National governments? The European Commission? Some combination of them? The question is urgent for
democratic societies because of some obvious realities: Online
platforms have become wide-open spaces for public and private debate; hatred is spreading through them with the help of
manufactured amplification; incitement to violence and discrimination seem to flow through their veins; and they have
become highly successful and profitable zones for disinforma
tion, election interference, and propaganda. It is also urgent in
non-democratic or transitional societies, like Myanmar, where
social media is the internet *and* the public sphere wrapped in
one. Whoever is in charge will have massive power over the
future of civic space and freedom of expression worldwide.
Given the stakes, democratic governance seems essential.

Outside China and Russia, American companies dominate
online space and the "moderation" of user-generated content in
it. (In techland, companies *moderate* content and governments
regulate it.) They make the rules that govern what users can post
or share and see. They provide commercial and political advertisers the ability to target their messages directly to individual
users, whose personal information has become an extremely

16   valuable commodity. They are, as the government-harassed founder of the Philippine news outlet Rappler, Maria Ressa, put it to me, "gatekeepers to the news," in which independent journalists had great faith, only to find company ignorance and denial conducive to manipulation and trolling. They are forums for human interaction, which can be meaningful and uplifting for hundreds of millions if not billions of people—but also can be deeply ugly, abusive, and abrasive.

Online entities, from the old message boards of the 1980s and '90s to blogs and traditional media outlets managing their comment threads, have always acted as gatekeepers of content. Today's platform behemoths take it many steps further: They have become institutions of governance, complete with generalized rules and bureaucratic features of enforcement. They have struggled to figure out how to police content at the scale to which they have grown. Often defensive, their business model involves acquiring user content and marketing what they learn about users (about us) to third-party advertisers. Their content policies, and their content policing, are nearly impossible to disentangle from their economic interests, even though the people who make and enforce the policies have, in my experience, a good-faith intention to do the right thing for their users.

This book takes a look at how the dominant American companies—Facebook, Google/YouTube, and Twitter—police their platforms. Of course, others police large platforms, too, including Chinese giants like WeChat and Russian sites like VK—but no others have the global power of these three. It is also a book about government plans to rein in Big Tech's control of public space, especially efforts by European authorities. The massive accretion of private power over public speech has justifiably unsettled governments, democratic and authoritarian alike. Authoritarians, of course, lack the constraints of legal and electoral accountability to hold them in check. Some want the platforms to block government criticism and basic reporting of such things as corruption and terrorism. In places like Turkey, research suggests that government pressure and demands for platform content takedowns have chilled individual expression and online search.

If, as in some gauzy glorified past, American law operated to protect individuals against monopolistic-minded companies, this would be a book that turned eventually to Congress and the president, maybe also the courts. But American legislators and policymakers seem structurally unable to adopt smart legislation. They are constitutionally myopic in their rigid understanding and politicization of First Amendment values. European governments and institutions, however, are playing the lead role in the democratic world in seeking to reclaim the authority to develop content rules for the internet, and those moves and rhetoric have implications worldwide. They could show the way toward rights-oriented regulation, or they could give cover to those who want to undermine rights in favor of protections against vague concepts like extremism and national security.

Outside the United States, the argument is direct: Policing is a public function, and government has a responsibility to get companies to tamp down on hate speech, terrorist content, disinformation, child sexual abuse, privacy interference, and political manipulation. While this is legitimate, in practice, attempts at regulation are paradoxically increasing corporate power— *American* corporate power—to be in charge of vast swaths of global public forums. Regulators demand adherence to rules concerning expression but have been unwilling or unable to think creatively about how public institutions, especially judiciaries, can incentivize compliance with the rights of users and can supervise corporate behavior; instead, they leave it to the companies to enforce and adjudicate—and often to censor.

Meanwhile, the activists, journalists, and academics who are often on the front lines of political debates have little input into the rules. Many feel squeezed between the overt power of the state and the covert corporate forces policing their content and shaping the information environment they work in. Nobody wants or expects a lawless environment, whether it's the law of the state or the law of the platform. But as corporations have gained greater control over public space, the human subjects of "content moderation" want to know the rules that govern the platforms and the secret accommodations that companies afford governments.

It's time to put individual and democratic rights at the center of corporate content moderation and government regulation of the companies. Around the world, the global standard is not, "*Congress shall make no law . . .*" but rather the Universal Declaration of Human Rights's Article 19 protection, "*Everyone has the right* to freedom of opinion and expression; this right includes freedom to hold opinions without interference and to seek, receive, and impart information and ideas through any media and regardless of frontiers." For many in the democratic world, their laws governing expression track the UDHR and its binding progeny, the International Covenant on Civil and Political Rights (a treaty ratified by over 170 states whose Article 19

grew out of the UDHR). Under treaty law, governments may
restrict expression where necessary and proportionate to protect legitimate interests, such as the rights of others, public
order, or national security, which can provide a basis for companies to deal with some of the ills of the contemporary internet.
If these were the standards that companies applied, rather than
the discretionary rules embedded in their terms of service, they
would have the capacity to make principled arguments to protect their users in the face of authoritarian and democratic governments alike.

Facebook CEO Mark Zuckerberg told an interviewer in 2018
of his search for shared values that could be acceptable to his
global community of users: "I've been working on and thinking
through [this question]," Zuckerberg said. "How can you set up
a more democratic or community-oriented process that reflects
the values of people around the world?" This is what people outside the United States often find so remarkable and, in its way,
arrogant and ignorant. Could he really only be struggling with
that in 2018, after all the content scandals of recent years? Did
he not know that *global norms* of free speech do exist in places
like the Universal Declaration of Human Rights? He has a global
platform, with users and activists whose principal reference
for rights is international human rights law, so why not look at
global norms?

Zuckerberg is not alone. It was only in August 2018 that
Jack Dorsey, co-founder and CEO of Twitter, admitted that
"our early values informed our rules" and "we need to root these
values in human rights." Until recently, American giants—their
policy officials and lawyers marinated in American law, institutions, politics, and culture—have virtually ignored the global

20 vocabulary and norms of free speech in favor of Americanized terms of service and community guidelines or rules. This is untenable, and they are starting to recognize it.

In place of what the companies offer now, digital rights activists often argue for something else: public recognition by the dominant companies that they have massive impact on the rights of billions of individuals and the societies in which those individuals live; company commitment to translate this acceptance into the norms that govern their platforms, namely a commitment to apply international human rights law; and a radically different approach to public accountability, especially public involvement in their rulemaking, publicly accessible data showing how they enforce their rules, and appeals systems for the hardest cases. They also need to adopt processes to ensure that local communities, far from the deceptively playful offices and baristas-on-demand of California, have a vested interest in the policing of the platforms—something they lack almost entirely today.

But this is not merely an industry-driven problem; it is a democracy problem. Governments need to encourage corporations to adopt transparent rules and enforcement strategies, perhaps even through binding regulatory requirements—but not through heavy-handed regulation of content or the fear of penalties that could undermine competition and innovation. Much of this book will underscore that, in democratic societies at least, the pressure on companies has led to an outsourcing of public roles to private actors, which amounts to an expansion of corporate power instead of constraints on it. I show how this is happening in some of the key areas of public concern: hate speech, terrorist content, and disinformation. Ultimately, I take away from these stories two sets of recommendations, one set calling for significant rethinking of how the companies moderate content on their platforms, the other calling for government regulation not to interfere with content decisions but to encourage that the platforms promote and protect the freedom of expression of all their users and the integrity of public institutions.

Platform Power

Uploaded to YouTube in May 2011, the video shows an adolescent boy's corpse, his body battered and burned, his eyes shuttered. A man narrates in Arabic while pointing out the body's many wounds: bruises, punctures, castration. Hamza al-Khatib was thirteen years old. It was the first video from the Syrian war that would influence public attitudes toward the government of Syrian president Bashar al-Assad, triggering outrage and mass protests. In the West, Hamza, reportedly detained while attending an anti-government protest in Daraa the month before, became "the face of the Syrian uprising," a "symbol of Syrian revolution," a life cut brutally short by a regime determined to retain power. The video had global impact, an introduction to the new power of social media and search platforms. Hamza's parents, who had consented to the publication of the video, wanted his terrible death to trigger just this kind of awakening of Syria under Assad.

As quickly as the video came up, however, YouTube took it down. Company policy prohibited sharing images of "dead

bodies or similar things intended to shock or disgust." The
video *is* shocking; it was posted *in order to shock*. Yet its value to
the public interest could not be denied. Complaints about the
takedown flooded in. Days after blocking the video, YouTube
unblocked it, adding an age-restriction warning.

YouTube polices its site, just as Facebook (and its photo-
sharing platform Instagram), Twitter, Reddit, Tumblr, Snap-
chat, Russia's VK, China's WeChat, and every other platform
hosting user-generated content does. They adopt, enforce,
revise, and often avoid what scholars increasingly refer to as
platform law. The blocking of the video of Hamza al-Khatib
puts the policing in sharp relief: How is YouTube or any other
platform to distinguish troubling images it wants to bar from
the site from those of extremely high public interest? Should
YouTube be the one making those decisions, and if so, on
what basis?

Hadi al-Khatib (no relation to Hamza) would also experience the power of YouTube. The Damascus-born activist
had worked with Iraqi refugees after the American inva-
sion and studied technology and information security in col-
lege in Damascus. At a time when the anti-Assad protests of
2011 were transitioning to civil war, Hadi had the skills and
interest to help foreign journalists maintain their *infosec*. However, it soon became increasingly difficult for journalists, local
and foreign, to operate in Syria at all. The government regularly
refused visas to foreign journalists, and those who did make it
into the country would, like countless Syrian reporters, be subject to threats and attacks if they departed from official minders.
Dozens of Syrian reporters were killed during the early years
of the war. American correspondent Marie Colvin was killed

24   in 2012 in an apparently targeted attack on the pop-up media
center from which she was covering the war.

In this environment of extraordinary danger for those
who collect and disseminate information, in 2011 Hadi and
some friends started the Syrian Uprising Information Center,
connecting people through a Facebook page and mapping the
uprising using Google Maps. Staying in Syria after 2012 meant
risking imprisonment, torture, and death, so he left to set up the
information center in Gaziantep, Turkey, a border town full of
exiled Syrians seeking to contribute to the protests from outside the country. He kept the information center up and running
until 2013, but it was constantly hobbled by hacking and false
reporting. Pro-government forces would game the reporting
systems of Facebook and YouTube, mass flagging information
as "graphic" so the companies would take it down. Like activists
worldwide, especially early in the social media revolution, Hadi
and his colleagues were winging it, and they did not know how
to respond. They tried to appeal to the companies but found it
nearly impossible to get through to anyone in Silicon Valley.
They moved the site to an independent server, only to be pursued by hackers, trolls, and censors there as well.

At the same time, across Syria, the internet was delivering
on its promise of cheap and democratized access to information and news, and the ability to share that information. Journalists, citizen reporters, and regular bystanders were all
capturing scenes of war, often on their phones, and uploading
them as quickly as they could to YouTube, often linking to Facebook and Twitter. Hadi knew many who were taking extreme
risks to share the material, and he knew it had value. There were
videos of conventional attacks on civilians that were not being

reported widely because of the dangers of entering Syria. There
were examples of torture, of the use of barrel bombs and chemical weapons, of summary execution of detainees by the government and by terrorist groups like ISIS. This was information
that not only highlighted the reality of the war but, someday,
could be used as evidence to indict a government's officials,
rebels, and terrorists for war crimes.

In 2014, Hadi and his fellow volunteers created the Syrian
Archive to capture as much as they could of these types of information. Initially they browsed Syrian YouTube channels and
downloaded relevant material as they saw it. But in 2015, they
built software that would crawl through YouTube and download
new material to the Archive's servers at periodic points each
day. By mid-2018, the Archive had already downloaded over 1.5
million pieces of digital content (though the process had been
so resource-intensive that they had been able to verify and cate-
gorize only about 4,500 images or videos).

Then came the policing. Starting in 2017, Hadi and his
team found that YouTube was deleting videos faster than the
Archive could download them, while videos the Archive did
preserve would later disappear. From the perspective of justice, this was an outrage: Footage of potential war crimes and
crimes against humanity should be protected from deletion,
verified as a matter of urgency, and shared with journalists and
the United Nations. Deletion undermines accountability, even
if that accountability amounts only to establishing a historical
record, or preparing evidence for criminal proceedings that will
not launch until years in the future, if at all.

YouTube saw it as somewhat more complicated than that.
Its Community Guidelines had evolved since the takedown

26   of Hamza's video in 2011. As with other companies, YouTube adopted what it presented as "common sense" rules meant to screen out from the platform sexual content and pornography, especially child exploitation and abuse, or content that is "harmful or dangerous," "hateful," "violent or graphic," harassing or bullying, threatening, or a misuse of copyrighted material. Some of these guidelines reflected the kind of brand that YouTube wanted to promote, fearing (probably correctly) that the advertising lifeblood of the platform would bleed out in the face of too much "difficult" or "objectionable" content. Some of the guidelines were as much the result of government regulation as public or advertising pressure, such as rules against "content that promotes terrorist acts, incites violence, or celebrates terrorist attacks."

YouTube places itself between the person uploading content and the public. Social media thus represents a new kind of speech police, determining what can be seen and what must be hidden. And they must do it at enormous scale: In 2008, about ten hours of videos were uploaded to YouTube every minute; by 2018, YouTubers were uploading nearly 450 hours of content every minute.

The enormous volume of uploaded content requires that the company rely on two tools to surface potentially problematic or illegal content: humans who comb through and report content, and algorithmic automation, or Artificial Intelligence. Ideally, flagged content would undergo human evaluation before it is taken down, whether it results from human or algorithmic flagging. But that's not always the case. Both human and algorithmic flagging can lead to mistaken deletions or blockings, or ones that activists or governments may simply disagree with.

Drawing the lines is hard. Many of the videos present troubling
images of violent death: certainly images that may be frightening for children or—in the eyes of some—celebratory of
the violence itself. YouTube may allow such material if it has
educational, documentary, scientific, or artistic value—they
call it "EDSA." But in the absence of context, it is often impossible for the tools of automation to distinguish EDSA content
from rulebreaking videos. Perhaps exacerbated by the growing
dependence on AI to police the enormous volume of uploads,
mistaken or contested takedowns have become a regular feature
of YouTube's efforts to police violent content that the public
has a strong interest in viewing. Juniper Downs, a former ACLU
attorney who heads up content policy for YouTube, admits, "We
don't always get it right."

Hadi understood YouTube's position, but its rules are
enforced in a manner that is opaque to him and his colleagues.
With the support of established digital rights organizations,
such as the Brooklyn-based WITNESS, he has been trying to
make the case to YouTube that the public and historical interest
in the Syrian Archive's videos strongly argues against takedowns. He told me, however, that even finding the right person
at YouTube to provide support can be nearly impossible. WIT-
NESS's Dia Kayyali, a supporter of the Syrian Archive and a
former advocate at the Electronic Frontier Foundation, has been
arguing for wider training so that those who upload videos know
how to include context and thus clarify that the material meets
the company's EDSA standards. But even then, algorithmic filtering tends to sweep in huge amounts of contextualized content.

It's also easy to wonder how much of the content deletion is truly a mistake. YouTube faces enormous pressure

28   from governments to remove content related to terrorism in any way. European governments and the European Commission want YouTube and other social media companies to take down "illegal" content within an hour, and the companies are loath to anger them, fearing the heavy hand of state regulation. Between trying to placate authorities and trying to serve the needs of activists like Hadi Al-Khatib, or parents of children like Hamza, YouTube walks a narrow path even as it tries to police its platform.

If the Syria stories speak to the perils of overzealous content moderation, Facebook's role in Myanmar speaks to another extreme—the inconsistent and weak enforcement of its rules. Over the course of six weeks beginning in the summer of 2017, the military of Myanmar (known as the Tatmadaw), with the support of Buddhist militant groups, forced hundreds of thousands of Rohingya Muslims to leave the country for Bangladesh. Thousands were murdered and raped. The UN High Commissioner for Human Rights called it a "textbook example of ethnic cleansing." Not long after, the UN Human Rights Council established a fact-finding mission to determine responsibility for the crimes. Along with its strong condemnation of authorities, the mission had another target of concern, which it summarized in 2018: "Facebook has been a useful instrument for those seeking to spread hate, in a context where, for most users, Facebook is the internet."

While Twitter and YouTube have a foothold in Myanmar, Facebook is dominant, used by almost everyone in the country who uses the internet—about twenty million people. Facebook has become a way for people across the country to share

news and information, in ways that were inconceivable under
the military regime of the past, which strictly regulated all
kinds of expression and media. Since the lifting of military
rule beginning in 2011, Facebook's entry and rapid populariza-
tion through its Free Basics platform—giving individuals free
access to Facebook but not the entirety of the internet—offered
people a different way of thinking about information and media.
The trouble was that expanding communications and access
to information also meant expanding the ability of nefarious
actors to use Facebook for hateful purposes. Tatmadaw officials
and militant anti-Muslim Buddhist groups used it to spread
content that reinforced Burmese discrimination and racism
against the Rohingya community.

Facebook provided an important platform for dissemination of this incitement, though in theory Facebook's rules prohibiting hate speech could have been deployed for positive
use. Militant figures and the Tatmadaw itself used Facebook
to disseminate untrue stories about Rohingya attacks on Burmese people and to foster an atmosphere of hate against the
Rohingya generally. The language was incendiary, calling for
the destruction of the Rohingya as a people, describing them
in language that brought to mind the dehumanizing rhetoric
of Nazi Germany against the Jews. Facebook failed to moderate these posts. Instead, mystifyingly, it took down posts
describing actual attacks against the Rohingya and suspended
a user group designed to tell the Rohingya where attacks were
taking place so that they could avoid them. While Facebook may
not bear the blame for the ethnic cleansing of the Rohingya, its
failures are tragic and epic, and it cannot avoid acknowledging
its role. In a country where even the leading figure, Nobel Peace

30   Prize laureate Aung San Suu Kyi, refused to condemn discrimination and violence against the Rohingya, whom the government denies citizenship, where journalists are imprisoned for exposing potential crimes against humanity, and where the law leans against protecting freedom of expression, social media can be part of both the problems and the solutions.

In April of 2018, an NGO coalition in Myanmar sent Mark Zuckerberg a letter, coordinated with other #DearMark letters sent from Sri Lanka and Vietnam. In it, the groups expressed deep disappointment in the platform. They wrote, "This case exemplifies the very opposite of effective moderation: It reveals an over-reliance on third parties, a lack of a proper mechanism for emergency escalation, a reticence to engage local stakeholders around systemic solutions, and a lack of transparency." Facebook, they alleged, failed to engage with civil society— those in the best position to help the company understand the nature of the threats in Myanmar—in any systematic way over the course of four years of escalating usage and escalating hate. The coalition called not only for better moderation of the platform, but for the hiring of more moderators (of whom there were very few, none in the country itself), for the improvement of escalation processes, and for transparency. A human rights consultancy commissioned by Facebook, and published by the company in November 2018, reached similar conclusions.

The problem for Facebook—and, more seriously, for Myanmar and other communities where the company has a substantial presence—goes well beyond the specifics of how to apply its Community Standards to specific branches of its empire. It could hire moderators who not only speak Burmese, but understand the politics, codewords, colloquialisms, and hidden meanings of online messages. It could have an actual physical presence in the country and have closer ties to the people whose speech it regulates, though this carries the risk of increased pressure from the government, whether by influencing the hiring of moderators or threatening company representatives with liability for failing to meet government demands. It could have more regular and deeper engagement with civil society actors in Myanmar.

It may very well be the case that Facebook offers something to the people of Myanmar that they would not otherwise have, and so its distance and foreignness may be tolerable, something to accept as an alternative to government control of the media. And yet, even if that is true, users in Myanmar still have little control over the rules that govern their posts and the posts of others they follow or friend. It feels to many like digital colonialism, and whether it is a long-term net-positive remains to be seen.

Beginning in early 2017, I started to receive direct messages on Twitter from journalists and activists in Kashmir, the highly militarized region that India and Pakistan have disputed and fought over for decades. A flashpoint for terrorism, government repression, and allegations of extremism, the fraught political environment of Kashmir is reflected on social media platforms. In times of public protest, the Indian government has shut down the internet and mobile telecommunications in areas where it has jurisdiction, a harsh and disproportionate response. It has also sought to block platforms, websites, news media, and other sources of information.

Increasingly I heard stories of Twitter users who would be reporting on conflict, or sharing information about protests,

32   or discussing threats they faced from the government, only to suddenly lose access to their account or find a tweet deleted. Twitter appeared to have withheld tweets and suspended accounts when users participated in discussions concerning Kashmir on the platform. Kashmiri users received notifications that informed them of this punishment either "in response to a legal demand" or "based on local law(s)."

People started to ask me for help, in my role as the UN's special rapporteur for freedom of expression, in which I monitor free speech worldwide and report to the Human Rights Council and General Assembly. They often reached out on Twitter itself to complain about the increasing account actions. While they blamed the Indian government, their anger toward Twitter was complex. They wanted to use the platform. When they lost access, Twitter would not explain why, or how to appeal, or whether an appeal would even be possible. Was it an allegation of hate speech? Terrorist content? Did the government make the demand? It may even have involved flagging by users who disagreed with a tweet, particularly in the case of coordinated flagging efforts. The users would not know which tweet or tweets led to their suspension, if indeed any of them did. They would not know if India presented any particular allegations and whether Twitter pushed back as a matter of local law or human rights law. I received countless messages complaining not merely about the suspensions but about being in the dark. They felt powerless in the face of an opaque and distant California power.

India has also done something else that many governments do: It has demanded that social media companies suspend accounts or take down content. This remains an enormous

problem for corporations worldwide. According to platforms' 33
terms of service and the logic of their businesses, they agree
to be bound by local law in the places where they operate or
where they are available. This should not be shocking to anyone.
A publicly stated failure to follow local or national law would
make it very difficult for them to operate; governments would
block access to them, make it difficult for platforms to engage in
the market, and possibly harass or even arrest employees in the
country. But that does not mean the companies lack leverage.
They are popular, and shutting them down often leads to ire
against the government concerned. As a result, corporations
often say that they require any government demands to be presented to them by normal legal process—the adoption of a law,
for instance, or a court order, or by order of some other independent legal authority. That may not be sufficient to protect
users where the courts lack independence, but it is at least one
layer of formal protection. Often, the process by which governments make demands of the companies is opaque and shrouded
in claims of privacy or national security. All of the major companies produce Government Transparency Reports to provide
aggregate data of government demands. But generally they are
difficult to parse and limited in what they really tell us about
their relationships with governments.

India has increasingly made account and content demands
of Twitter, particularly related to Kashmir. According to Twitter's transparency report, from July to December 2016, India
made 96 removal requests, and Twitter did not act on any of
them. From January 2017 to June 2017, India made 104 removal
requests, but Twitter again did not withhold any accounts or
tweets during that period. Then from July 2017 to December

34   2017, India made 144 removal requests, in which 800 accounts
were specified. The report states that, of the 144 removal
requests, Twitter withheld 17 accounts and 32 tweets in the
same period. Something clearly changed in 2017, and the reasons are not clear.

Mario Costeja Gonzalez had a problem with Google in his native
Spain. If anyone searched for him by name, the first result would
link to a government notice in the Barcelona-based *La Vanguardia* newspaper announcing the attachment of his property
to satisfy a debt. Even fifteen years later, that notice marked him
like a digital scarlet letter. He had pulled his finances together
and thought the link interfered with his ability to work and
get credit. So he sued Google and its subsidiary, Google Spain,
demanding they delete the link to *La Vanguardia*—and he won.
Google appealed all the way up to the highest court of the European Union. That court, the European Court of Justice, held
in May of 2014 that search engines like Google must, upon
request, ensure that irrelevant information about a person—
information "no longer necessary in the light of the purposes for
which it was collected"—does not appear in name-based search
results. The court acknowledged that rules for public figures
may vary, but it found that the individual's interest in delinking
would "override, as a rule, not only the economic interest of the
operator of the search engine but also the interest of the general
public in having access to that information."
 Google Spain, as the case that gave birth to the "right to be
forgotten" is known, provides Europeans with the right to ask
a search engine like Google to delink or de-index a website
from name-based search results if it meets the conditions of

irrelevance just noted. It is up to Google, or any relevant search 35
engine, to adjudicate in each instance whether the claim meets
the standard set out by the court. Google, the largest by far of
the search engines, enables individuals and companies to submit
requests and it then evaluates the claims and makes decisions
based on the information submitted. In 2018, Google, in its periodic Right to be Forgotten Transparency Report, noted that it
had evaluated 2.4 million URLs that Europeans requested be
delisted since 2014, 43 percent of which were determined to meet
the standards of *Google Spain*. Put another way, Google actually
denies more than half of "RTBF" requests, only a tiny fraction of
a percentage of which are appealed to a national data protection
agency or court. Private individuals made up 89 percent of the
requests, and of those who were not private individuals, about
20 percent were government officials or politicians and 15 percent of them were non-governmental public figures; 40 percent
were minors. One startling piece of data was reported in Google's
own study that it subjected to peer review: Just one-fourth of 1
percent of all requesters (1,000 individual requesters) made up
15 percent of all URLs requested to be delinked. Google asserted
that these were principally law firms and reputational management companies. As the study put it, "the RTBF can lead to a
reshaping of search results for certain individuals."

Google Spain privileges privacy rights over freedom of
expression; indeed, as a coalition of NGOs noted, it does not
even mention the right to freedom of expression under the
European Charter.

As such, the case may have harmed basic principles underlying the public's right to information. It left open the possibility that historically important data can simply be buried.

36   It outsourced some hard questions about the intersection of European privacy law and freedom of expression to private entities. From another vantage, however, *Google Spain* can also be characterized as Europe's effort to restrain Silicon Valley and impose upon it some responsibility. In fact, Google dominates public space across Europe more than Facebook or Twitter does. In the course of the proceedings, several countries and the European Commission urged the court to adopt strict rules to enable Europeans to ensure that Google would observe European rights. While these submissions are framed according to the legal requirements of the court, they are also obvious attempts to ensure European control over public space and individual rights.

Google Spain points in a direction that the situations in Myanmar, Kashmir, Syria, and elsewhere do not: It points to the use of democratic institutions, the tools in place where rule of law prevails, in order to restrain the operations of corporations. It results not only from a legal environment allowing such challenges but also one that enables individual agency in the face of corporate power. Europeans have tools to constrain not only the way the platforms collect and process personal data, but they have tools to constrain how the platforms govern public space. For a variety of reasons, including the priority given to privacy rights on the continent, Europeans have acted aggressively to regulate online privacy, as the recent entry into force of the General Data Protection Regulation, or GDPR, attests. They have acted less aggressively on content regulation, although the European Commission's focus on hate speech, terrorist content, and disinformation suggests that may be changing. They have strong public institutions, administrative bodies, and

national and constitutional courts. As a result, Europeans have
the tools to pressure the platforms to shape up.

In developing countries, individuals lack that access.
They are distant geographically and they are weak institution-
ally. This has facilitated the companies' blasé attitude toward
smaller markets. After all, what do they have to fear? This attitude means that individuals and civil society organizations
must work exceptionally hard to advocate for control over their
platforms. They come as supplicants rather than, as in Europe,
potentially powerful consumers. It's an enormous power that
corporations have, and if they act irresponsibly, they need to
own up to the consequences and remedy the damage they have
done and still do.

The Internet
Comes to
Washington

The Vindicator serves South Liberty County, Texas, a community northeast of Houston with a population of about 75,000. It's the kind of small-town paper, with its news and classifieds and local look at national issues, that anchors the public life of many communities around the United States. In the summer of 2018, its editors had the perfectly civic-minded idea of posting the Declaration of Independence to the newspaper's Facebook page in bite-size chunks in the twelve days leading up to the Fourth of July.

All was going well until July 2. That day, the five paragraphs of the relevant section of the Declaration did not appear. Paragraph 31, the last of those five paragraphs, asserts this about the king of England:

> He has excited domestic insurrections amongst us, and has endeavoured to bring on the inhabitants of our frontiers, the merciless Indian Savages, whose known rule of warfare, is an undistinguished destruction of all ages, sexes and conditions.

The Vindicator's editors received a notice from Facebook
indicating that the post violated the company's content rules.
Casey Stinnet, the paper's managing editor, was perplexed.
Reporting the takedown to his readers on July 2, he noted,
"While *The Vindicator* cannot be certain exactly what triggered
Facebook's filtering program, the editor suspects it was most
likely the phrase 'Indian Savages.'" And then, in a wry follow-on,
he noted, "To be honest, there is a good deal in that passage that
could be thought hateful."

Facebook lucked out to have had as thoughtful a victim of
content removal as Casey Stinnet. Stinnet presumed that this
was not a politically minded takedown. It was an automated
removal and he imagined that a human reviewer would see
the problem and restore the relevant sections of the Declaration. But it wasn't easy. For one thing, he didn't know how to get
Facebook's attention, a problem common to users worldwide.
But worse, he felt that publishing the remainder of the Declaration, if found to have further problematic language, could
lead *The Vindicator*'s Facebook page to be taken down. And that
would be a very big problem, because the paper—like so many
local papers across America—relies on Facebook for its dissemination and sharing of articles; it has become central to its business strategy at a time of declining support for local media. It
was a "quandary," Stinnet said, even if he could enjoy the "very
great irony that the words of Thomas Jefferson should now be
censored in America."

Several outlets picked up the story, including the libertarian
website Reason. A public outcry was inevitable, along with
serious Facebook embarrassment, but the following evening,
Stinnet was happy to announce that Facebook unblocked the

40   offending language and emailed him to admit its mistake. Vindicated, Stinnet said, "We never doubted Facebook would fix it."

The problem for Facebook, as it turned out, was not Stinnet or *The Vindicator*, but the Republican Congress.

The Vindicator story made its way to Washington and into a hearing of the House Judiciary Committee. A few weeks after the snafu, Republican congressman Bob Goodlatte, an apt name for the chairman of a hearing with companies that offer their employees free artisanal espresso, called to order a meeting to hear what Silicon Valley companies could tell Congress about their "content filtering practices."

Goodlatte began by telling the story of *The Vindicator*. "Think about that for a moment," Goodlatte said. "If Thomas Jefferson had written the Declaration of Independence on Facebook, that document would have never seen the light of day. No one would have been able to see his words because an algorithm automatically flagged it, or at least some portion of it, as hate speech. It was only after public outcry that Facebook noticed this issue and unblocked the post." The accusation from Goodlatte and the committee Republicans went something like this: The companies are ready to censor even the foundational documents of the American experiment.

Throughout Goodlatte's story time, content policy teams from Facebook, Twitter, and YouTube listened patiently. They awaited their turn to show that Goodlatte was wrong: that they don't respond merely to public outcry, that they don't target conservatives or liberals or anyone else along the political spectrum, that they have rules, policies, standards, guidelines, technologies, and procedures they try to apply neutrally. They were not there to talk about the Declaration of Independence and

Thomas Jefferson. They were there to show that they have carefully thought through how to moderate the huge volume of content posted to their platforms worldwide and that, when they
make mistakes, they fix them as soon as they can.

First up was Monika Bickert, the lead manager of Facebook's
content policy. Bickert, Facebook's oft-quoted Vice President for
Global Policy Management, has been with the company since
2012. A former federal prosecutor and the company's lead on
counterterrorism, Bickert has earned the respect of colleagues
inside and outside the company. She is known to be smart,
fair, extremely well prepared, and eager to get the rules right,
not only for the company but for the public impacted by the
platform. Her testimony reflected all the tropes of Facebook's
brand. "Community" appears nearly twenty times in her six
pages of prepared speech. (Mark Zuckerberg is said to be per-
sonally committed to the idea of Facebook as a community, even
as people throughout the industry often roll their eyes at and
mock a term that seems, in the context of a two-billion-user
platform, at once creepy and silly.)

While committing to free expression, Bickert noted a
struggle over "how to keep our community safe and the dialogue
on our platform healthy" in the face of challenges like harassment, bullying, hate speech, bots, and disinformation. Since at
least 2012, Facebook has referred to user safety as its "top priority." Facebook, in her telling, seemed less a neutral conduit for
ideas and information than a benign camp counselor, aiming
to "bring people closer together by encouraging more meaningful connections." She expressed contrition ("we won't get it
right every time") and diligence ("we learn from our mistakes
and are always working to improve"), while introducing steps

42   the company was taking to make sure their content review was robust and accurate. "Partnering" was the watchword, whether to "ensure we can most effectively serve our diverse community" or to "limit the reach of false news."

Juniper Downs appeared next. Downs has managed global policy at YouTube for years, joining Google the same year that Bickert joined Facebook and bringing her civil liberties background to the development of a range of content policies. It's a background that involves not only ACLU-style defense of speech and due process but also the protection and promotion of children in at-risk situations. She and Bickert have even co-taught a course at Stanford Law School on free speech on the internet. Far from the company bureaucrat one might imagine representing such a dominant company, Downs presented YouTube (and its parent, Google) less as the convener of a community than as a steward of a user-empowering platform for access to information. Google merely *supports* "the free flow of ideas" with "tools that empower users to access, create, and share information." *Users,* not community, are at the core of her message, although the rules that govern the platform are in fact called *community guidelines.* User empowerment means "choice, opportunity, and exposure to a diversity of opinion." Her prepared testimony did not once use the words "safety" or "dialogue" but emphasized that the platform's guidelines aimed at "keeping YouTube free from dangerous, illegal, or illicit content" to make sure that YouTube "protects our users."

Nick Pickles took up the last slot. Unlike Bickert and Downs, Pickles has a background in British electoral politics. He ran for Parliament as a Tory in a safe Labour constituency in 2010 and

then headed up campaigns for a scrappy but effective British   43
privacy rights organization, Big Brother Watch. Now Twitter's "senior strategist" for public policy and a recent transplant
from the London office to Twitter's San Francisco headquarters,
Pickles offered yet another message: "Our purpose is to serve
the public conversation." Less explicitly community-driven
than Facebook and less focused on the individual's right to
information than Google, Twitter came off, in Pickles's testimony, as committed to a public role—in other words, neither
a walled garden of community members nor a place for one-off
research assignments or entertainment, but an avowed participant in and shaper of *public* space.

But Pickles also appeared conflicted, something of a turn
from Twitter's self-proclaimed early role as zealous protector
of individual free speech. It was that role that gave the platform the reputation as an accountability-free zone for harassment and misogyny and Nazis and Alex Jones, a reputation the
company has sought to shed—particularly since a neo-Nazi
in Charlottesville, Virginia, killed Heather Heyer in August of
2017. Torn between beliefs that censorship will not "solve political or societal challenges" and that the platform must be "a safe
space for our users to share their viewpoints," Pickles emphasized that the Twitter Rules are about censuring bad behavior—
not "ideology or a particular set of beliefs."

Bickert, Downs, and Pickles answered questions from
the committee for the better part of three hours, though more
often than not they were used as props while the members took
turns making political points about their opponents and social
media. Unlike the UK Parliament's digital economy committee,
which held a probing and professional hearing with the same

44   individuals in Washington in February 2018 and issued a serious report in July, the House Judiciary Committee showed itself to be unserious. The committee members either asked very basic questions or, as was the aim of the Republicans who initiated the hearing, focused on narrow partisan questions of how conservative voices are allegedly mistreated online. The committee did not consider the core question of company content moderation: Given the hold they have on public space, should social media platform owners' rules be wholly within their discretion, based on business and perceived user needs, as corporate owners define them? Or should those rules be subject to public norms of free expression? Does online space suggest the possibility for restrictions that we might not tolerate offline? We accept that issues of competition and privacy require public regulation and accountability. Should that apply to expression as well? If so, given that the platforms are public and dominant, what should be the source of those rules?

The hearing was a lost opportunity, the questioners unprepared, the environment politicized. The year 2018 had provided hints that some members of Congress wanted to move beyond the political posturing and address the real problems posed by the platforms. Senator Mark Warner issued a white paper that summer with thoughtful ideas aimed at regulating disinformation, responding to foreign manipulation, protecting democratic institutions and processes, and protecting user privacy. It's possible that a differently configured Congress could address these issues. But based on Washington's recent track record, it seems unlikely to take the kinds of broad steps toward platform regulation that Europeans have been talking about. Regulation may be coming, but not from Washington.

Still, for those willing to listen, the hearing was illumi-   45
nating. The witnesses showcased the often obscured reality
of how bureaucratic and rule-oriented the giant social media
companies have become. The public and members of Congress
may begin with the premise that many of the companies lurch
from crisis to crisis and end up with a kind of seat-of-the-pants
approach to determining appropriate content on their platforms. And that does happen, much more often than it should.
But it's not the norm that the companies set out to establish.
They highly regulate user-generated content on their platforms.
The biggest of the companies are bureaucracies, adapting lawmaking qualities to the work they do on content. They may not
always be very good at it, but they are serious about moderating
what people can say and share and do on their platforms. They
have to make fine distinctions between the disturbing content
that they all allow and the threats that they prohibit; between
the insult that is kosher and the hate speech that is not, between
legitimate journalism depicting horrors of the world and groups
seeking to incite those horrors.

Close to their moments of conception, each company developed
terms of service to make clear that users sign up to the platform on its terms, according to its discretion, based on its rules.
From the American giants to Russia's VK to China's WeChat
and everyone else, users agree to abide by the law of the platform. We have all mindlessly clicked through terms of service,
by virtue of which we agree to observe the standards they set
out for what we might express, whether through video, text, or
image, whether in a post or a comment or a tweet or a note or
whatever. For Twitter, it's the Twitter Rules. For YouTube, it's

46 Community Guidelines. For Facebook, it's Community Standards. These are the standards that guide company decisions in crafting the platforms they want to present to their users, to their advertisers, to the governments in the jurisdictions where they operate. Within those standards, the platform owners also require users to comply with local law, and each company has policies for how they respond to government requests for content or account actions. Platform law involves company rules related to everything from abusive behavior and harassment to impersonation, threats of violence, disclosure of private information, sexual content, and nudity.

In their early days, the rules for all the platforms were spare, particularly on issues like hate speech, a notoriously difficult subject to define (and, in the United States, not generally subject to government regulation absent incitement to imminent violence or connection to an otherwise established crime). Kate Klonick, a law professor at St. John's University in New York, has shown in detail how those who developed the first iteration of community standards saw the platforms as American creations integrated into and dependent upon an American free speech culture. American and European laws also provided the companies with the room to moderate the content on their platforms without any fear of liability. This is known among companies and lawyers and advocates as the problem of intermediary liability, and, generally speaking, the intermediaries—like "platform," the word itself connotes a non-editorial role when it comes to content—are not liable for the content that their users generate and post. Section 230 of the Communications Decency Act immunizes internet companies from liability in the United States related to their policing of content. The European E-Commerce

Directive protects companies from liability in their roles as conduit for or host of information generated by users. Other jurisdictions, like India, have similar rules, protecting platforms
from liability as long as they did not have notice of illegal content posted by their users. It also immunizes the companies from
any liability for *taking down* content that might be fully lawful and
legitimate in a given jurisdiction. In short, the platforms have the
freedom to make their own content rules. For companies and free
speech advocates, this power to regulate has been foundational to
everything that followed: a freedom to adopt standards, to decide
what's appropriate, to be the regulators of their own spaces.

The earliest framers of company rules did not connect them
to any particular legal tradition other than the loosely understood values of the First Amendment of the U.S. Constitution—
more speech is good for business and good for the users, unless
it's speech that harms the platform, harms users, or deters
others from joining (which, of course, is not a First Amendment
standard). Their collective view at the outset was that they were
building platforms for people to connect with one another or
share information; they were not thinking about the billions who
would join them as they grew so rapidly. The business incentive
was obvious: More participation multiplies the data they collect about their users and increases that data's value to advertisers. The nascent companies reflected a kind of intuition about
principles of free expression and the companies' perceived need
to protect their perceived identities. In 2008, Google's deputy
general counsel, Nicole Wong, known within the company as
the Decider, noted astutely that the company should observe its
users rights but that it, too, had independent First Amendment
rights to design and develop its platform and brand.

Astonishingly rapid growth forced the companies to confront the reality that they would have to moderate user-generated content and establish rules about what people could share and say on their platforms. They all adopted basic rules to prohibit obvious abuse, such as bullying and misogynistic attacks, but they were also notably weak in their enforcement. They often failed to provide users with the tools to protect themselves, and even where they did, some users saw a transfer of responsibility from the platform to the victim. Journalist Charlie Warzel has made a career out of highlighting how often the companies fail to deal with fundamental rules against abuse and harassment. His "A Honeypot for Assholes" article in 2016 became an instant classic, showing that Twitter's approach to misogynistic attacks was notoriously weak not just at the vast scale of contemporary Twitter but even in the platform's early days.

The Vindicator gives us the opportunity to consider one of the common rules that all the platforms try to enforce: the norm against hate speech. We can find out how the companies have articulated the rules over time, what the rules look like across the platforms, and whether the rules have foundations in some legal tradition or they are just made up as platform owners face public outrage and controversy.

Presenting itself as jealously guarding public free speech norms, Twitter did not have any rule pertaining to "hate speech" until at least 2015 (and even then not expressly). By mid-2018, it prohibited what it called hateful *conduct*:

> You may not promote violence against or directly attack or threaten other people on the basis of race, ethnicity, national

origin, sexual orientation, gender, gender identity, religious affiliation, age, disability, or serious disease. We also do not allow accounts whose primary purpose is inciting harm toward others on the basis of these categories.

The Twitter Rules then note examples of prohibited content, such as references to mass murder involving protected groups, behavior that would "incite fear or spread fearful stereotypes about a protected group," and "repeated and/or non-consensual slurs" of groups or "other content that degrades someone." It's a vast and open-ended set of proscriptions.

YouTube has been policing hate speech since at least October 2006. "We encourage free speech," the site's early Community Guidelines said, but [emphasis in original] "we don't permit **hate speech** which contains **slurs** or the **malicious use of stereotypes** intended to attack or demean a particular gender, sexual orientation, race, religion, or nationality." Today it clarifies that slurs and stereotypes without more are not proscribed, but it will block "content that promotes violence against or has the primary purpose of inciting hatred against individuals or groups based on certain attributes." There's a fine line, YouTube says, between proscribed hate speech and other forms of objectionable speech, and it adds that "not everything that's mean or insulting is hate speech." Some hate speech may be excepted from blocking if it meets educational, documentary, scientific, or artistic criteria.

Until early in 2012, a full eight years after its founding, Facebook said very little on the topic other than that it "does not tolerate hate speech." It added, "it is a serious violation of our terms to single out individuals" based on prohibited categories

50 like race, national origin, religion, gender. It was only in 2015 that it fully revised the policy, claiming that it would remove hate speech, defined as "content that directly attacks people" based on a protected category; to disallow a presence for "[o]rganizations and people dedicated to promoting hatred"; and permit the sharing of hateful content only where it is for the "purpose of raising awareness or educating others." By the middle of 2018, Facebook introduced its hate speech principles with a policy rationale: "We do not allow hate speech on Facebook because it creates an environment of intimidation and exclusion and in some cases may promote real-world violence." It claims to ban organizations and individuals involved in "organized hate." The company also added some granularity, distinguishing, for enforcement purposes, three tiers of severity, from "dehumanizing" speech that refers to protected persons as, for example, "filth, bacteria, disease, and feces" or "animals that are culturally perceived as intellectually or physically inferior" (Tier 1), statements of inferiority, contempt or disgust (Tier 2), or calls for segregation or exclusion based on a protected status (Tier 3).

Over the short lives of these platforms, they have progressively tightened their rules across all areas of content: increasing specificity, tightening, restriction, and additional explication. All three companies moved from generic proscriptions to defining the term as involving attacks, such as inciting violence or hatred against individuals based on a protected characteristic. More than in the past, users and governments can see in the rules and guidelines how the companies define hate speech and make arguments, based on those rules, about what they think the companies ought to take down and leave up.

And yet it is often difficult to understand corporate decisions under those rules except in the most obvious cases, since
the companies do not release anything like a kind of case law
about their judgments. Hate speech is a notoriously difficult
concept to nail down. Human rights law provides that governments may restrict expression, which could conceivably include
hate speech, if it interferes with the "rights of others," and that it
should prohibit "advocacy of national, racial, or religious hatred
that constitutes incitement to discrimination, hostility, or violence." That legal proscription is uncomfortably broad, especially for American lawyers, largely unschooled in human rights
jurisprudence—unlike their counterparts around the world.
Users and governments have a difficult time knowing how the
rules are actually applied.

This has been true across all of the platforms. How platform rules are implemented, who makes them, how the terms of
service violations are treated—all have remained opaque, apart
from a handful of scholarly studies or reports. For this reason,
Ranking Digital Rights, a leading organization advocating for
platform transparency, has noted that companies disclose "the
least amount of information about how *private* rules and mechanisms for self- and co-regulation are formulated and carried out."

In their early years, it would have been an acceptable
response to say: *Hey, these are private companies! They're not governments! Who cares what rules they adopt? Join or don't join, stay
or leave.* Before they became global forces dominating public
space worldwide, these companies were competing with others
for users. They could be idiosyncratic, protecting their users'
rights but experimenting in a kind of cocoon of rulemaking and

52   enforcement while in the process of maturing into major global institutions.

That no longer pertains to the kind of platforms at least these three—Facebook, YouTube, and Twitter—have become. Their decisions don't just have branding implications in the marketplace. They influence public space, public conversation, democratic choice, access to information, and perception of the freedom of expression. They can no longer hide behind the curtain of corporate competitiveness. They have to acknowledge their unusual, perhaps unprecedented, roles as stewards of public space.

Humans and Machines

Content moderation is hard ... because it is resource intensive and relentless; because it requires making difficult and often untenable distinctions; because it is wholly unclear what the standards should be; and because one failure can incur enough public outrage to overshadow a million quiet successes.
—Tarleton Gillespie, *Custodians of the Internet* (2018)

If the early content standards were highly subjective in their enforcement and their framing, companies have matured to a place where their rules, even if written in a colloquial and accessible voice, have the power of law on their platforms. They are subject to a seemingly never-ending set of tweaks and edits and occasional rewrites, all through corporate bureaucratic processes that involve product and policy managers, lawyers, engineers, executives, communications specialists, and government relations types.

No company captures the lawmaking quality of content moderation better than what Monika Bickert has described as

54 Facebook's biweekly "mini-legislative session," where the company's content teams address speech policy questions and make fine distinctions about how they should regulate the platform.

It's the late spring of 2018, and I join one of these Content Policy Forum sessions as an invited observer. Facebook asked that I not publish the substance of the meeting but agreed that I could write about their approach. While I will not detail the specific decisions made in the meeting I attended, I will try to give a sense of the process.

About twenty Facebook employees gather at 9:30 a.m. on a Tuesday in *Finding Dory*, a conference room in Building 23 on the company's vast campus. Some twenty-five other employees stream in from across the Facebook diaspora, including another part of Menlo Park (*Proportional Response*), Dublin (*Hi Diddly Ho*), Washington (*American President*) and London (*Come Come, Mr. Bond*). One joined by laptop from what appeared to be Amtrak's Acela line between New York and Washington. In total, somewhere around fifty Facebook employees were participating, mostly young, dressed down, smart, focused, and seemingly drawn from elite schools and government institutions in the West. It is a snapshot of what Facebook's legislators are like, and they are much more serious, much more public-minded, and much more impressive than HBO's *Silicon Valley* might suggest.

A young man chairs the meeting, giving the impression that he's got to keep things running efficiently toward a conclusion at 10:30. That gives us an hour. He explains the process, though I am the only outsider in the meeting who needs the explaining. There are a lot of *recommendations*. He has three queued up for discussion and approval, after which the team will prepare

another set of recommendations, this time for implementation
about two weeks from now.

An employee streaming in from Dublin presents the first
issue for discussion. The question up for debate focuses on the
rules associated with political Facebook pages that have repeatedly promoted or hosted content inconsistent with Community
Standards—principally hate speech.

Facebook calls these groups politically "cross-checked"
pages—they tend to be high-profile or popular pages requiring
more than one level of evaluation before the company takes
action against them. Regardless of how the illicit content appears,
Facebook will take it down once it has notice of it—and count it
against the number of violations against a page. Facebook does
not typically suspend or delete a page immediately. It gives the
administrators opportunities to deal with the problem. Repeated
failure of an administrator to deal with the problem can result in
Facebook deleting the page; in the case of hate speech, the number
of violations that would lead to such a result depends on whether
it is Tier 1, 2, or 3. In the case of pro-Brexit page Britain First,
for instance, Facebook found that "they have repeatedly posted
content designed to incite animosity and hatred against minority
groups, which disqualifies the Pages from our service." After one
final warning, they were unpublished. This is also what happened
to InfoWars in August of 2018.

The question for Facebook has long been: Are they providing
enough warning to such users? Do administrators of these
pages understand adequately the rules governing them? This is
a serious problem for any of the companies—how to deal with
accounts that are avowedly political, involving public-oriented
debate, while striking against content that involves expression

56   the rules prohibit. These kinds of pages seem to put Facebook in a no-win position: If they leave up the page, they anger opponents who see hateful content or disinformation; if they take it down, they offend free-expression advocates who do not think the rules very clearly articulate hate speech standards. There is also the ever-present potential that advertisers could find the association with such pages deeply problematic.

Richard Allan, the most senior Facebook employee in Europe and a former member of the British Parliament, placed the hate speech problem in the context of political debate in an interview with Channel 4 television in the summer of 2018:

> This is not a discussion about money. This is a discussion about political speech. People are debating very sensitive issues on Facebook including issues like immigration currently and that political debate can be entirely legitimate. It can also slip over into hate speech. And we are working very hard to try and understand that line and be very clear with people where the line is. If you slip over into hate speech, we will remove your content. But we don't want to be over-censorious of legitimate political debate. That's the decision we need to make and I do think having extra reviewers on that when the debate is taking place on the site of a political party, absolutely makes sense and people would expect us to be careful and cautious before we take down their political speech.

The Shadow (Ha-tzel), an Israeli hard-right rapper, provides an example. The Shadow's Facebook page has repeatedly used the kind of language that incites anti-Palestinian hate. In 2014, The Shadow himself posted on Facebook asking his followers to demonstrate against "the real enemy among us: the radical left"—a suggestion that led some to attack peace activists at a rally. A further issue for Facebook is whether The Shadow or someone on his communications team can control the comments on his page. Should the administrator be responsible for those comments? According to Facebook, the answer is yes.

Team Dublin now prompts a recommendation to address the warnings an administrator might get before the company takes down a page, which Facebook ultimately adopted and published an overview of in August. With the vibe of a law school seminar, I try to keep up with the questions and discussion:

Does it matter how serious the underlying violations are?

What about administrators who don't receive the notifications of violations? It's common for administrators not to read their inbox and get messages from the company. How do we ensure that they have actual notice and we give them a chance to fix a problem?

Where does the administrator see the message concerning a violation? Will the administrators get a violation sent to their inbox? An interstitial on the page?

Will the administrators have an opportunity to appeal? What will that appeal look like?

These are exactly the right questions you would hope Facebook would be asking itself, and the team answers questions for a good half hour. It is clear that this forum is the end of a lengthy process, one that has involved internal review and the

58   solicitation of views from experts outside the company. The participants make a genuine effort to get it right—to find the right rule for the company, to try to bring it into alignment with some ideal of fairness balanced with brand needs. They are impressive at both the group and individual level. But that cannot obscure the reality of the legislative role they play for billions of users, who themselves lack input into rule development.

The group finds consensus on the change and the responsible team members will move toward implementing the new policy. And while there seems to be more interest in discussion, the chair notes that it's time to move on.

On January 6, 2018, the German news outlet *Suddeutsche Zeitung* published a stunning first-person account by someone at the front lines of content moderation. Moderators do the difficult work of deciding whether content violates company rules. Burcu Gültekin Punsmann, the author, exposed the ugly and terrible reality of a human being who has to see thousands of beheading videos, torture scenes, instances of animal cruelty, threats of violence, and other hateful or abusive content.

Before Punsmann, few had exposed this daunting work *from the inside*. Sarah Roberts, a professor of information science at UCLA, had led the way, detailing in field-defining scholarship how poorly paid moderators—most of whom were hired by outsourcing companies in places as varied as Berlin, Manila, the Bay Area, Lisbon, and other corners of the globe—had the punishing job of reviewing and deleting content that violated platform rules. Content moderators were seen as a front-line force protecting users from everything from images of beheadings and child abuse to the language of bullying, hate,

and incitement. They had the secondary role of protecting
the self-image of the platforms as democratic and community
space rather than cesspools of horrid content. It was what one
Motherboard story called "taking the trash out," and what one
documentary (in which, in disclosure, I appeared) referred to in
its title as *The Cleaners*. *The Guardian* newspaper had also published leaked slides showing what the moderators were trained
to see as violating the rules, when they should delete the content, when they should leave it up, and when they should run the
matter up the ladder to Facebook itself.

I met Punsmann at a café in Berlin in the summer of 2018.
She was not a typical moderator. Hired by Arvato, a subsidiary
of the Bertelsmann conglomerate to which Facebook outsources
content moderation in Germany, Punsmann took an entry-level
job to review Turkish content, even though she held a doctorate
from Sciences Po in Paris and worked for many years on human-
itarian assistance and conflict resolution for the United Nations
and NATO. Her coworkers at Arvato were, according to her, typically educated and multi-lingual but without advanced degrees;
they were mostly young, new immigrants, and often desperately
in need of work. She was between jobs, and when she learned of
an opportunity at Arvato, she was curious, even though it only
paid minimum wage. She found the two-week training inter-
esting, even intellectually stimulating, and decided to see what
it would be like.

But on the job, she found that the gore and cruelty she saw
at work infected her dreams. There was a shocking amount to
review; she understood from Arvato that the requirement was
for moderators to handle about 1,300 reports a day, a figure that
Facebook disputes.

60   As corroborated by an undercover operation at another Facebook contractor in Dublin, and broadcast by the UK's Channel 4, Punsmann and other moderators were set up at computer interfaces that gave her access to online policy documents (rules, hypotheticals, etc.), an in-box for messages from Arvato, and a dialog box noting her break time (five minutes per hour, half hour for lunch). The screen would alert her if she didn't move her mouse for five minutes. Coming in, she would log in and get into queue. At that point, content began to appear, giving her the option to delete, to ignore, or to escalate to a supervisor or a Facebook employee in the rare circumstance where an answer was difficult. The documentary *The Cleaners* provides a disturbing current of narration inside the head of a content moderator: *delete, delete, ignore, delete, ignore, ignore, delete....* Escalation, she suggested, was rare and discouraged.

Content made its way to the queue when either a user or a platform algorithm flagged it for review as problematic. Let's use an example: an image of a young girl, naked, screaming in tears, soldiers behind her, a burning village in the background. This was, of course, one of the signature images of the Vietnam War: the photograph of nine-year-old Phan Thị Kim Phúc running naked on a road near Trảng Bàng after a South Vietnam Air Force napalm attack there, taken by Associated Press photographer Nick Ut, who was awarded the Pulitzer Prize for it in 1973. It was famously blocked by Facebook when it was posted by a Norwegian newspaper in 2016. That image—a nude girl—would almost certainly trigger Facebook's automated system to flag and block it as a violation of the platform's rule against nudity. If the algorithm had not alerted a moderator to it, a human might: All platforms use some kind of user flagging tool. However it

gets to the content moderator, once the image is flagged, the
moderator must decide whether to delete or allow it to remain.
She doesn't have a lot of time. Does it fit into an exception, such
as journalism? Newsworthiness? Awareness-raising? She may
seek guidance from subject matter experts at Arvato or escalate
to the company's content specialists, but the general pressure is
to decide oneself.

In her essay, Punsmann noted that "reflection is not encour-
aged." In person, she told me that Arvato was in fact even more
direct than that: Content moderators are told, she said, "Don't
think too much." Facebook's directives were to decide on the
basis of guidance and *not* to get hung up on context. She felt
powerless in the face of the never-ending flow of human misery
she witnessed at her workstation.

She wondered, "Did those social media tools subcon-
sciously encourage people to overcome all inhibition by
destroying all social filters and moral barriers?" She couldn't
imagine this conduct as *social,* and yet individuals posted such
trash with the paradoxical aim of *gaining* followers, building
an audience, finding some form of community, no matter how
warped. She concluded her essay with the following:

> The only power that the content moderator has, is to delete
> a post. On rare occasions, I could send a notification to the
> person highlighting that the post was cruel. I wished I could
> use the function more often. I dreamed often of being able to
> communicate with the person behind the post, but there was
> no time. There is a need to educate society. This requires a col-
> lective effort. The protection that the content moderators try
> to offer is only enabled by the reports generated by the users.

The degree of secrecy and level of confidentiality around the practices of content moderation doesn't help. The burden and responsibility cannot rest only on the technology companies. But they can support the development of online communities.

Punsmann highlighted what the companies sought to keep closed from public view: the development of rules, the enforcement of standards, the impact on those who make and implement the rules. For social media companies that are aiming to advance access to information, connect members of a community, or contribute to a public conversation, this opacity is hypocritical. As long as it continues this way, governments and users will react to company decisions with the same kind of anger and blame and politicization that each high-profile takedown generates.

With the volume of content coursing through all of the platforms, the companies have had to identify ways to surface content that poses the most difficult problems under their rules or under the national laws where they operate. Two tools dominate. The first, one that has been with content moderation since early in the lives of the platforms, is users notifying the company of alleged rule violations. This is typically known as flagging. It is hard to imagine the platforms developing without flagging, which offers users some measure (or at least a feeling) of influence or input over their platform experiences. But at the same time, flagging is subject to serious abuse. It is easy for groups to coordinate flagging to harass and troll users—triggering actions such as suspensions or takedowns of posts even where no violation is at issue. Platform owners have not been good at adjusting

to the abuse of flagging, but it remains a tool that would be diffi-   63
cult to imagine them getting rid of, especially given how, particularly for targets of harassment and abuse, it empowers recourse
to remedies.

The other tool is machines—algorithmic identification of
violating content, collectively placed under the rubric of Artificial Intelligence. AI has worked well for some problems, such as
child sexual exploitation, where there is a consensus about what
constitutes a rule violation. In general, AI may work better for
images than text. It allows for companies to determine what kind
of content should be deleted or reviewed, or how to order and
curate news and search results, or friends or tweets or stories to
recommend, "training" the software over time to know the difference between the acceptable and the unacceptable.

The public's impression of AI is that it is machines run
amok, but it is really human programming and the leveraging
of that power, which is a massive one for corporations. The
machines have a lot of difficulty with content, especially text,
with all the variations of satire and irony and misdirection and
colloquial choppiness that is natural to language. They have difficulty with human difference and have facilitated the upholding
of race, gender, and other kinds of biases to negative effect. Even
worse, as the scholar Safiya Noble argues in her book *Algorithms of Oppression*, "racism and sexism are part of the architecture and language of technology." And all of this is not merely
because they are machines and "cannot know" in the sense of
human intelligence. They are human-driven. We often do not
know the answers about meaning, at least not on a first review.
The programmers have biases, and those who create rules for
the programmers have biases, sometimes baked-in biases

64   having to do with gender, race, politics, and much else of consequence. Exacerbating these substantive problems, AI's operations are opaque to most users and present serious challenges to the transparency of speech regulation and moderation.

All of the companies are using AI and recommitting to it. Mark Zuckerberg has made clear that he expects increasing shares of Facebook's content moderation to be handled by machines. He said in November 2018, the "single most important improvement in enforcing our policies is using artificial intelligence to proactively report potentially problematic content to our team of reviewers, and in some cases to take action on the content automatically as well." They're not ready to handle the toughest challenges, he acknowledged, but Facebook and YouTube in particular are clearly banking on AI solving significant content challenges as the volume of content remains astronomical (and may continue to expand). It is a risk to speech if they fail to build into their tools the fundamental rights that users have not only to express themselves and participate in the public life the platforms offer but also to know the grounds for content and account decisions taken against them. At the moment, it is not clear that the platforms are prepared for that, seemingly incentivizing AI's operation more than user rights.

And worse, company confidence in "proactive moderation" is feeding into government imaginations of the power of AI to filter all sorts of expression at the point of upload. Repeatedly, European leaders express the belief that AI can solve public problems, such as hate speech, terrorist content, disinformation, and copyright infringement. This belief is feeding into the Age of AI, which risks an age of content regulation largely hidden from the tools of public accountability.

Wir schaffen das!

The way Heiko Maas saw it, Facebook betrayed him. That sense of betrayal ultimately changed German law and shook up the way democratic governments battle for control of the rules governing online speech.

It was mid 2015. The remains of the Arab Spring—particularly the chaos following the wars in Libya and Syria—led hundreds of thousands of migrants to seek protection in Europe. Asylum seekers were making their way to Europe over deadly smuggling routes across the Mediterranean Sea and through lengthy treks across Turkey and into southern Europe. Thousands of lives were lost along the way. Echoing Barack Obama's "yes we can," German chancellor Angela Merkel boldly assured Germans at the end of that August that they could welcome one million refugees. "Wir schaffen das!" *We managed so many things before, why not this?*

Not everyone agreed with Merkel's approach, especially not the German far-right. Some took to the streets, with anti-migrant riots and the firebombing of refugee centers led

66 by skinheads and other neo-Nazis. Others took to social media to target refugees, migrants, and German politicians and journalists. Research has highlighted some correlation among anti-refugee posts on Facebook and actual attacks on migrants or their property. In the midst of a European-wide immigration debate, social media seemed to many to have become a meet-up for neo-Nazis and an amplifier of the kinds of speech that are illegal under German law (such as criminal defamation and insult, defamation of religious institutions, Holocaust denial, and disseminating depictions of violence).

Enter Maas, then the German Minister of Justice and Consumer Protection. A key figure in the government and the opposition Social Democratic Party, Maas supported Merkel's refugee policy. He reflected a widely held view among German leaders that the hate spreading across the country risked loss of life and damage to Germany's stability. At a UN conference in September 2015, Merkel, caught on a hot mic, challenged Facebook's Mark Zuckerberg about it directly. Skinheads and others filled with racist rage had long been in Germany, but their message could be isolated and their tactics dealt with by traditional law enforcement tools. There was something different here: hatred spread virally, without the moderating factors of traditional media and the sunlight of societal disapproval. Social media companies, German officials believed, could not be safe spaces for violations of German law any more than a *bierhalle* could be.

Maas focused on Facebook. In a late August letter to Facebook's European headquarters in Dublin, Maas expressed dismay that the company was not effectively policing speech on its platform. It wasn't merely that the speech on the platform could be in violation of German law; he believed that Facebook failed to enforce its own rules that prohibit hate speech. German citizens were telling his office that they could not understand how nudity (legitimate under German law) would be taken down but vile hate speech, often inciting hostility or violence, would not. Justifications for action or inaction would not be given. Facebook's claims to be evaluating and taking down unlawful content and accounts, Maas wrote, were a "farce." He demanded they meet.

Facebook's spokesperson in Germany responded carefully, avoiding responsibility for the problems Maas identified: "We are very interested in an exchange with Federal Minister Maas about what society, business, and politics can do together against the spreading xenophobia in Germany." Twitter and Google were invited as well, and the participants met. Together they created a joint task force that, in Maas's conception, would push the companies to limit expression that was inconsistent with German law or with their own terms of service. The Task Force Against Illegal Online Hate Speech, which also included a handful of anti-hate advocacy groups in Germany, quickly agreed to a Code of Conduct. Released on December 15, 2015, the code (optimistically named *Together Against Hate Speech*) decried the way "public debate degenerated to xenophobic and racist hate speech." The companies committed to remove hate speech quickly upon notice. They would try to make it easier for users to report hate speech and would review those reports in less than twenty-four hours.

The Code of Conduct gave everyone a quick victory. Maas welcomed the agreement, saying social media could not become a "funfair for the far right." In the German government's view, the companies promised not only to meet their obligations in Germany but to help reduce the spread of hate at a destabilizing

68   moment in German political life. The companies avoided liability under German law—they committed to make an effort,
not to achieve a specific outcome. And since they already prohibited hate speech under their own rules, they weren't obligated to do anything other than what they already claim to do.
(This is a classic American approach to treaty negotiation—
magnanimously accept all commitments that do not require a
change in law or behavior.)

Months passed, and Maas saw incremental change at best.
His team thought the companies were playing a game of hide-
and-seek, with limited transparency into their operations. Maas
himself felt betrayed by the companies' (especially Facebook's)
failure to achieve real advances in taking down hate speech. So
Maas directed Justice Ministry lawyers to put a hard edge on the
soft law of the Code of Conduct: real obligations with real penalties for failure to comply. By the spring of 2017, with a draft law in
hand, Maas claimed that "networks aren't taking the complaints
of their own users seriously enough." If the companies wouldn't
police German legal violations as they promised, he would force
them to do so under the threat of stiff sanctions.

On March 14, 2017, Maas released his proposed law, the
Netzwerkdurchsetzungsgesetz—or NetzDG, the Network Enforcement Law. While the Code of Conduct relied on the companies'
good-faith efforts to stamp out hate speech on their platforms
in Germany, NetzDG relied on the power of sanctions. It made
obligatory what the code only suggested: The platforms would
be under a legal requirement to remove content that violated
specific provisions of German law. (German government lawyers believed that they were already under such an obligation,
as a matter of German and European law, once they had notice

of "illegal" content.) NetzDG would require that "manifestly illegal" content be deleted within twenty-four hours of notice; other illegal content would require deletion within a week of notice. German law prohibits certain forms of insult and defamation, the dissemination of Nazi symbols, public incitement to crime, and other kinds of expression that typically involve careful legal review to know whether they are actionable or not. This would now be the legal responsibility of the corporations. And if they failed to institute procedures that enabled them to take down unlawful content, they could be fined millions of Euros—systematic violations could result in up to a fifty million Euro sanction. The law also created new obligations of disclosure to ensure that the public could see exactly how the companies were meeting the requirements of the law.

German free speech activists, international experts, and the companies objected—as did I, in my role as the UN's special rapporteur on freedom of expression. We focused on two related problems of principle: First, NetzDG demands that companies take down content without the involvement of public authorities. If the terms of service and other content policies neatly overlapped with German law, this might not be a problem, since a content takedown under platform rules would naturally cover the legal violations as well. But that's not always the case. Hate speech under company rules, for instance, is rooted more in loose corporate standards than any one country's laws, while Germany's law on insult has no analog in company policies. Even where there was overlap, NetzDG was asking private corporations to stand in the place of courts and public prosecutors. They would be judge and jury not only of their own standards (as one would expect) but also of German law, bringing with them

70   not the public accountability of the courts but the private incentives of what one senior European Commission official in Brussels described disparagingly to me as "the profit-making beasts."

And this led to the second objection. As a Twitter employee once put it to me, "The economic incentives to keep content up do not exist." The steep penalties for noncompliance, applicable only to the largest social networks (i.e., the three involved in the Task Force exercise), incentivize the takedown of content and the suspension of accounts. The law does not include any countervailing pressure to keep legitimate content up, and there were no penalties for the takedown of satire or political commentary or anything else. The platforms would almost certainly take action against borderline or legitimate content that violated no rule in German law, just to be certain of not violating the law.

Despite these objections, the German Bundestag adopted NetzDG in the summer of 2017, and it went into force as of the beginning of 2018. It is hardly the last word in German regulation of the internet. It may be just the first salvo. Insiders told me that they expect further review of NetzDG to consider rules that would require the companies to adopt appeal processes where there are objections to content actions, which some of them are already doing. They may involve broader government supervision of the companies' content policies. One government lawyer suggested that the NetzDG would be improved by requiring the companies to develop better tools of automation—"upload filters"—to capture illegal content even before a user posts it, much as China's platforms automatically censor content. NetzDG, in other words, could be the vehicle and the model for governments to impose new rules not only of content regulation but of prior restraint.

Not long after NetzDG became law, Heiko Maas moved on to head the foreign ministry. But his sense of frustration—the feeling that companies would not do what he believed German law and society demanded them to do unless forced by the power of law and legal sanction—is shared across Europe, a kind of alienation from the power that enormous American companies wield over the public space across the Atlantic.

Momentum was also picking up for action at the European level. Within weeks of the November 2015 ISIS attacks in Paris, the European Commission announced the creation of "a public-private partnership to detect and address harmful material online" and "extremist abuse of the internet." The Commission initiative would aim to get the major internet companies to commit, in the words of the EU's Commissioner for Justice and Consumer Affairs, Věra Jourová, to "eradicate" online hate speech, first through an EU Code of Conduct on hate speech similar to the one negotiated in Germany. From March to May 2016, a Commission team negotiated a code with Twitter, Facebook, Google, and Microsoft. The closed-door negotiation, largely conducted by emails that a Brussels-based NGO coalition, European Digital Rights (EDRi), obtained through a freedom of information request, excluded other relevant tech actors, such as Apple, blogging platforms, messaging apps, European tech companies, and media. It also excluded civil society, governments, and academic experts. The emails show an almost too-easy negotiation, a kind of backroom effort to enlist companies in the enforcement of European law. On May 31, flanked by company reps in Brussels, Jourová introduced the Code, linking it not to attacks on migrants, as Heiko Maas had, but to terrorism in Europe.

The Code of Conduct seemed merely to restate what the companies already did—or at least claimed to do in their rules, such as observing national laws and prohibiting incitement to violence and hate speech. The companies promised to "review the majority of valid notifications for removal of illegal hate speech in less than 24 hours and remove or disable access to such content, if necessary." The "if necessary" does a lot of work here, because it left within the company's discretion whether to take action against content or users. The Code reinforced the power of the companies to make these kinds of adjudications without the supervisory role that might be offered by public institutions.

Prominent human rights organizations dissociated themselves from the process, and Article 19, a leading global free speech organization, strongly critiqued it. The Center for Democracy and Technology questioned the lack of a court or other independent arbiter of illegality, leaving individuals subject to excessive takedowns, the absence of remedy, and generally opaque processes involving government flaggers of Code-violating content. The Commission responded by disputing that the Code could lead companies to *overregulate* their platforms and take down content not subject either to European hate speech law or terms of service.

Meanwhile, company resistance to legal obligations infuriated some officials. "Because the companies are American," one Commission official told me, "we have problems. We have no influence—only if we regulate. American law enforcement has dialogue with the companies that we don't enjoy."

Another European official could not hide disdain for American companies and American valorization of speech over

other rights, such as protection against potential violence and   73
discrimination.

"Words lead to violence," this official told me. "Weimar and radio led to Auschwitz. American companies say you cannot show causality and *blah blah blah*, but you can see the relationship between hate speech online and what's happening in the real world. Until today—well, the main stakeholders are not there, those *harmed* by the violence."

"Also, if you want to protect speech on the internet," this official continued, "you have to draw lines on hate speech."

Who should draw those lines? I asked.

"Democracy rules, not the internet companies. There is a problem for democratic legitimacy to do it this way [the way of the Code of Conduct]. It should be decided by law. The digital rights organizations are right that this is about fundamental rights. . . . But I would say that the reason it should be *law* is that law could and would go further. The Code of Conduct is weak and wishy-washy."

This sounded to me a lot like NetzDG.

"It must be [decided by] democracy, not technology. There's a responsibility beyond the internet. For rights activists, it's always just inside the internet, but the politics regarding the internet today is general societal politics. . . . The bodies of democracy will have to own up to a view of regulating the internet. The question isn't what's best for the internet—that's just one tool of many things to have in society—but it's not the most important political job. Poor and rich, left and right—they are more important than what's good for the internet."

The Commission would later take steps toward a European-wide version of NetzDG that would require all member states

74   to impose certain kinds of requirements on company content
moderation. Even with the Commission reporting improved
removals of the undefined category of "hate speech" content,
some Brussels leaders ramped up accusations of online law-
lessness. Jourová said, "We cannot accept a digital Wild West,
and we must act." The Commission has been formally calling
for prompt removal of hate speech on the platforms. Indeed, it
wants the companies to move toward "proactive measures to
detect and remove illegal content online." This is code for upload
filters, a form of prior restraint that relies upon automation
and Artificial Intelligence tools to disable users from posting
content based on algorithmic assessment. Across Europe, the
momentum for regulation is strong.

Choose Your Side

In May of 2017, Darren Osborne watched a BBC miniseries, *Three Girls,* which dramatized a real-life child abuse sex ring, the so-called Rochdale grooming case. After *Three Girls,* Osborne became wholly focused on the national and religious origins of the British Pakistani perpetrators, even though he had not been known by his family or friends to hold racist ideas. He turned to the internet almost immediately, drawn toward Islamophobic hatred and disinformation and incitement. He read posts by noted white supremacist Tommy Robinson, such as, "There is a nation within a nation forming just beneath the surface of the UK. It is a nation built on hatred, on violence, and on Islam." Hardly a month after the BBC program and the beginning of his journey into Britain's online racist back-alleys, Osborne headed toward London in a van he had rented in Cardiff the day before. He had one aim: to ram his truck into marchers at the annual pro-Palestine Al Quds Day March, which he assumed would achieve his goal of killing Muslims. Foiled by security when he attempted to enter Central London, Osborne looked

76   elsewhere, finally happening upon the area around the Finsbury
      Park mosque in North London. He drove his van directly into
      a crowd, killing fifty-one-year-old Makram Ali and injuring
      many others.

      The presiding judge at Osborne's trial, Justice Bobbie
      Cheema-Grubb, offered this interpretation of how Osborne, in
      a relative instant, became the man who killed in Finsbury Park.
      Addressing Osborne directly, she said:

> You became incensed by what you believed to be the inadequate
> response of political leaders and other authorities to such
> criminal conduct [as depicted in *Three Girls*]. Your research
> and joining Twitter early in June 2017 exposed you to a great
> deal of extreme racist and anti-Islamic ideology. You were rap-
> idly radicalised over the internet encountering and consuming
> material put out in this country and the U.S.A. from those
> determined to spread hatred of Muslims on the basis of their
> religion. The terrorist atrocities perpetrated by extremist Isla-
> mists fueled your rage. Over the space of a month or so your
> mindset became one of malevolent hatred. You allowed your
> mind to be poisoned by those who claim to be leaders.

      Osborne, alleged at trial to be chronically unemployed,
      depressed, possibly suicidal, and an alcoholic, may have been
      the perfect receptacle for the propagandists operating racist
      accounts on Twitter, YouTube, and Facebook. Although Jus-
      tice Cheema-Grubb addressed him as an individual with
      agency—*you allowed your mind to be poisoned*—she implied
      that the internet enabled his radicalization. If we accept that
      online racism contributed to Osborne's turn to violence and
      hatred, how should governments and platforms address that

contribution? What should corporations and governments do about the Darren Osbornes—but also about the Tommy Robinsons—of the internet?

The British police have alleged that many of the recent acts of terrorism attempted in the UK, whether by white supremacists or by Islamists, have had "an online component." Mark Rowley, the UK's National Lead for Counter-Terror Policing and assistant commissioner of the Metropolitan Police, emphasized that Osborne radicalized on a diet of "large amounts of online far right material." Rowley did not limit his concern to social media, as he called out the traditional media for giving disproportionate attention to people like Robinson and militant British Islamists like Anjem Choudary.

Social media companies have set up rules to police and remove terrorist content and terrorist organizations from their platforms, adopting broad definitions so that they can be responsive to governments. They have developed Artificial Intelligence technologies and automated hashtag databases that identify terrorist content and enable its nearly immediate takedown, and they talk endlessly about the possibilities AI offers to limit terrorist content. They are connecting with police and security services through the United Nations and through an industry initiative known as the Global Internet Forum to Combat Terrorism. They have agreed to the Code of Conduct on hate speech. All of this involves the companies removing content or sanctioning accounts.

But governments continue asking for more.

In his first trip to the UN General Assembly as president of France, in September of 2017, Emmanuel Macron joined Theresa

78   May, the British prime minister, for an event she hosted on "preventing terrorist use of the internet." May had laid the groundwork for a joint British, French, and Italian statement calling for international cooperation "to prevent the dissemination of terrorist content online and the use of the internet by terrorists to radicalize, recruit, inspire, or incite." She deployed the loose language in which political leaders talk about "dangerous content," and became specific when demanding that the companies "go further and faster in automating the detection and removal of terrorist content."

It was Macron, however, who captured the strategic direction of government efforts and their essential characteristic: an expectation that private companies would exercise public responsibilities. He made the point clearly and threateningly enough that, if the leaders of Silicon Valley were listening, they should have been at least a bit anxious. In a with-us-or-with-the-terrorists way, he said, "There are those who fight for our values, the freedom and security of our fellow citizens, and there are those who decide to play the game of terrorists. Choose your side."

Governments around the world, democratic and authoritarian alike, have been demanding that social media and search companies solve the problem of terrorist content online. Govern your space, or we will assume you're on the side of the terrorists.

All of the key actors in the debate over policing the internet agree that incitement to violence should be removed from online platforms. It is prohibited under most legal codes worldwide, whether national or international, including human rights law. There are variations around the imminence of the violence, and

many governments prohibit incitement to hatred and discrimination as well, as human rights law provides. (That's a notable
distinction from American First Amendment law, which does
not permit the government to prohibit incitement to hatred or
discrimination.)

Beyond incitement, there is debate over what else should be
subject to censorship, and governments have been reluctant to
clarify. The UK, France, Spain, and others have adopted criminal laws that prohibit encouraging, glorifying, or apologizing
for terrorism, all of which are at the far margins of government
authority under human rights law. Governments could not
order the removal of merely "troubling" speech in the absence
of a basis in national law, so they ask companies to do it instead.
They avoid the bitter fights that would come from adopting in
their domestic laws definitions that, because of their breadth,
would be susceptible to legal challenges in their courts under
constitutional and human rights law.

While this characteristic outsourcing is a common thread,
governments have adopted two models of internet policing
of terrorist or extremist content. The first involves the police
work of so-called Internet Referral Units (IRUs), and the second
involves Macron-style warnings. Both models involve pressure,
one passive aggressive and the other simply aggressive.

IRUs have spread globally from the UK to the European
Union and beyond. The British government has been monitoring social media since at least 2010, when Scotland Yard
established the Counter-Terrorism Internet Referral Unit
(CTIRU), the first of its kind. I had expected the doors to the
CTIRU to be closed to me. But on an unusually hot July morning,
at their invitation, I made my way to the headquarters of the

80   CTIRU, in a thirty-story building that towers over Earls Court and West Kensington in London.

The CTIRU does not have the power to *order* takedowns. It can only request them. It polices social media in the broadest colloquial sense of the word, reviewing major platforms every weekday from 7:00 a.m. to 7:00 p.m. They are a shadow government to the content moderators, those with real takedown authority like Burcu Punsmann and those at Arvato and other contractors working at computer stations in office buildings in Berlin, Manila, and elsewhere. About two dozen police officers scour the internet for terrorist content, using keywords that they will not divulge, while fielding reports of alleged terrorist content sent from private individuals from across the UK.

The CTIRU does not publish the rules it follows to determine whether content is reportable to the companies, but it does allow individuals the opportunity to report what it calls extremist or terrorist content. If the CTIRU determines that the reported content is illegal or in violation of a company's terms of service, they will refer that to the company and ask that the content be taken down. ("The longer the email, the less robust the case for takedown," one social media company employee quipped to me.) One officer told me that the companies did not even speak to the CTIRU until around 2014. (A well-informed former Google employee assured me this is not the case.) It was around then that videos of beheadings and other brutal crimes surfaced in increasing numbers online. Advertisers panicked, and the companies opened up. Early on, the CTIRU focused on things like the ISIS propaganda magazine, *Inspire*, as well as incitement, bomb-making instructions, and messages by

jihadis contained in *nashids,* or ballads. Its officers, I was told,
struggle with the things that free speech advocates would hope
they would struggle over—how to distinguish a wild rant or a
sarcastic disingenuous "threat" from an incitement to violence,
how to distinguish the student scientist blowing stuff up for scientific or other reasons from terrorism training. CTIRU officers
claim that part of their role is to "safeguard the open internet."

As of April 2018, the CTIRU claimed to have successfully
requested the removal of 304,000 "pieces of terrorist-related
material," but they seem not to collect data about the nature of
those removals, the kinds of content involved, or the companies
at issue—they evidently do not maintain statistics about the
nature of their work. The CTIRU's work does sometimes trigger
criminal investigations.

IRUs cannot force platforms to take down content, but they
may be vehicles for governments to apply pressure on companies
to remove offensive content that doesn't actually violate laws or
their terms of service. They take advantage of open-ended platform standards to insist upon takedowns. AccessNow, a global
advocate for the application of human rights law to internet
speech, has characterized IRUs as "not just lazy, but extremely
dangerous."

If governments believe content to be problematic or dangerous or harmful, removal of that content should be subject
to basic democratic principles: adoption of new laws by regular legislative process, subject to judicial or other independent challenge, demonstration by government of the necessity
and proportionality of the action. But with IRUs and outsourced
content moderators, that is simply not happening.

———————

Across the Channel in Brussels, one European Commission official told me in the summer of 2018, "Terrorism content is not a problem. The companies deal with it, often within an hour, and hashtagging is the way forward." I wondered about that, because at the same time, Commission officials were preparing to increase the pressure on the platforms to take down what they describe as terrorist content.

In fact, companies have developed AI technologies to enable the removal of terrorist content within the hour of upload. Reposted terrorist content, once it is in a specified "hash database" accessible to all the companies, may be deleted or blocked within moments of attempted upload. Companies have taken these steps under public, economic, and political pressure. Company definitions of terrorism, in their content rules, were broad enough to encompass anything that governments might demand.

Still, European governments continue to express dissatisfaction with company behavior and the reach of European law to impose responsibilities on them. In September 2018, after a protracted debate among Commissioners, the Commission proposed to move beyond the soft law of voluntary commitments. Věra Jourová argued that "we should have absolute certainty that all the platforms and all the IT providers will delete the terrorist content and will cooperate with the law enforcement bodies in all the member states."

"Absolute certainty" is fantasy. With the bar placed that high, governments are setting up the companies to bear political responsibility for any future terrorist attacks. They will be blamed by governments because they did not catch terrorist

content or take it down fast enough. This is liability-plus—the
hard reality of financial sanctions to be threatened on the companies plus the political reality that there is no easier scapegoat
for a European official than the American companies that host
so much of the public discourse in Europe. The companies are
playing along, talking up their use of AI and hashing to remove
terrorist content, because they do not have much of a choice.

In the fall of 2018, the Commission proposed a regulation
that would expand the responsibilities of companies to take
down material said to incite terrorist acts and to actively monitor user-generated content on their platforms. But instead of
involving public authorities—courts or other independent
agencies—to determine when an act aims to incite or "glo-
rify" terrorism, it asks that companies make that determination for each of the twenty-eight member states of the European
Union. Its breadth and vagueness are problematic. This is not
like child sexual abuse, for which there is a consensus around
imagery that clearly and objectively meets a concrete definition.
Rather, it is asking companies to make legal decisions, and fine
ones at that, about what constitutes the elements of terrorism,
of incitement to terrorism, of the glorification of terrorism.
Companies are policing content that meets these criteria, rather
than the usual institutions of democratic governance.

"Arbiters of Truth"

There is an epidemic sweeping the world. If left unchecked, it could be worse than all the plagues that the world has recorded put together. It is a clear and present danger to global peace and security. It is a threat to democracy. It is the epidemic of fake news. Mixed with hate speech, it is a disaster waiting to happen.

—Lai Mohammed, Nigerian Minister of Information (2018)

Shortly after Donald Trump's election, the *New York Times* fingered social media as the culprit that produced this shocking political event, blaming the "liars and con artists" who "hijack" platforms with "fake news." The *Times*, like most everyone else not working at one of the social media companies at the time, didn't know as much as we would come to know about online disinformation: the role of Russia and its troll factories, the degree to which disinformation influenced voters and outcomes, the technology available to corporations to counter it, the factors that distinguish it from other kinds of data. But that didn't stop the paper from pleading with Facebook, which it noted tweaks its

algorithms and its spam filters all the time, to do the same with   85
disinformation. "Surely," the paper concluded, "its programmers
can train the software to spot bogus stories and outwit the people
producing this garbage." Could programmers really train com-
puters to find fake news if humans couldn't?

The *Times* wasn't alone in its concern. Others around the
world were beginning to grapple with the problem of online disinformation. Across the Atlantic some months later, in a glassy
building housing the European Parliament in Brussels, Marietje Schaake worried that the "technological revolution" led by
American social media companies threatened European democracy. A creative, insightful, and energetic parliamentarian from
the Netherlands' liberal D-66 party, Schaake had long stood
with human rights activists in their advocacy for open and
secure digital platforms. Notwithstanding her pro-American
and pro-tech credentials, Schaake reflected a widely held concern that Europe was losing control of its civic space to companies that, in the process of perfecting algorithms "for optimal
advertising revenue," had become vehicles for "propaganda and
hoax." "No one wants a Ministry of Truth," Schaake said during
parliamentary debate in 2017, "but I am also not reassured when
Silicon Valley or Mark Zuckerberg are the *de facto* designers
of our realities or of our truths." Schaake would tell me of her
concern that companies lacked even the basic elements of legal
accountability for their content policies, and were increasingly
capable of operating globally with virtually unlimited discretion and little government oversight.

Later, on the margins of the annual UNESCO World Press
Freedom Day, held in 2018 in Accra, Albert Antwi-Boasiako,
the cyber-security adviser to the president of Ghana and an

entrepreneur and leader in the country's technology sector, shared with me his sense of the risk posed by social media companies dominating public spaces. He told me that he sees online fabrications as a national security issue, with the potential to destabilize peace in the country. A supporter of company self-regulation, he wanted an awareness campaign so that people would have the tools to distinguish fake from genuine, opinion from fact. Unfortunately, he added, company cooperation with Ghana is "not too great." A small country without the market power enjoyed by North Americans or Europeans, "we don't have the feeling that they are committed to our needs."

Kwami Ahiabenu, a tech and media expert at Ghana's *penplusbytes* NGO, shared this perception, noting that companies are focused more on access than content in Ghana. Disinformation, Ahiabenu told me, spreads quickly from WhatsApp (the dominant platform in Ghana) to mainstream media, which is always hungry for "juicy stories." Ghana has not had a serious problem with disinformation yet, but that did not stop the country's Inspector General of Police from warning in 2016 that he would consider shutting down social media on election day if he thought it necessary, a warning widely criticized.

Damian Collins, a Tory MP in the United Kingdom, felt much the same as Schaake and Antwi-Boasiako. Throughout 2017 and 2018, Collins led a parliamentary investigation into the role of social media in the referendum that led to Brexit. The Cambridge Analytica scandal, in which the British company infamously obtained massive amounts of personal data from Facebook users without their consent, and which Facebook appeared to hide from the public and regulators, jolted Collins's

investigation and energized its members. In the summer of
2018, shortly before his committee released a damning report
accusing both Facebook and Cambridge Analytica of serious
violations of user privacy, Collins met with me in his office at
Portcullis House in Westminster. He could not hide his frustration with Facebook.

"They downplay every revelation," Collins told me, adding
that Facebook is "especially reluctant to disclose information." They are not publishers in the traditional sense, he said,
but neither are they neutral platforms, given how they curate
and engage with political content. He saw room for all the platforms to do better with illegal content, but found disinformation to be a difficult gray zone. He envisioned a kind of traffic
light system that allows users to see, for instance, the country
of origin of information, but he also imagined the potential for
transparency-focused regulation. I could sense his uncertainty,
but also his determination to find legal mechanisms to force the
companies to do better.

Not one of these individuals is anti-American; they are certainly not anti-technology. None wants to ban social media. They
are policymakers with genuine concerns about the way social
media amplifies disinformation and propaganda—material that,
before social media and search engines came to dominate how
we seek and receive information, would have had an extremely
limited niche audience. They see online disinformation, as
researchers at the Oxford Internet Institute put it, as "a critical
threat to public life." They share a sense that the companies are
not doing enough to deal with disinformation. While opposed
to excessive regulation, they all came reluctantly to the conclusion that it may be time for government to step in.

While much of the world was freaking out over Donald Trump's election, the attitude from Facebook was one of sangfroid. Two weeks after Election Day, Mark Zuckerberg updated his status on his Facebook page and began by recognizing that "a lot of you have asked what we're doing about misinformation." "The bottom line is," he said, "we take misinformation seriously. . . . We've been working on this problem for a long time."

We know now that Zuckerberg was not on top of this problem. In his November 2016 post, he explained that Facebook's approach relied on the community to identify fake information. It sounded as if he were blaming the community: "Anyone on Facebook can report any link as false," he noted, "and we use signals from those reports along with a number of others" to root out misinformation. Facebook penalizes it, he added, just as if it's clickbait or spam. And anyway, he asserted, there's not a lot of misinformation on the platform to worry about.

Zuckerberg's position failed to mollify the public and did little to placate those calling for action. His response likely made things worse, as it demonstrated a real disconnect from the concerns of governments going into major elections, especially in Europe. The platform, from the start, has followed its founding motivational motto—move fast and break things— with a public relations protocol that said, "Oops, sorry." "There is more work to be done" indicated both recognition of a problem and the company's inability to solve it quickly—and perhaps its unwillingness to devote the resources governments demanded. Zuckerberg said that Facebook would push forward on stronger detection using "technical systems"—meaning Artificial Intelligence—so that they could highlight false

information even before a user flags it. The company would
make reporting fake news easier. And it would *listen* by trying to
learn from media fact-checking programs.

But really, he concluded, "I want you to know that we have
always taken this seriously."

The public record did not support Zuckerberg's assertion.
Facebook had maintained a public-facing news blog for years,
and until late 2016, false information did not make an appear-
ance as a subject. This could be because the public lacked
interest, and Facebook tends to respond to public attention and
concerns. But only after Trump's election did the news blog
light up with stories about news feed and disinformation. From
then on, particularly in 2018, Facebook's steps indicated quite
clearly that it did not have a serious program in place to deal
with false information. What's more, the company knew it was
behind. In the first major post about what it called "hoaxes and
fake news" in December 2016, Facebook did not allude, as Zuckerberg had, to great amounts of work demonstrating that it took
the problem seriously. Instead it introduced "first steps we're
taking to improve the experience" of its users. And the steps
were modest, considering what we know now: easier reporting,
flagging stories as disputed, informed sharing, and interfering
with spammers' financial incentives.

The theory behind Facebook's approach seemed sound at
the time. In the absence of public information concerning what
Facebook knew about alleged Russian interference in the U.S.
presidential elections, it was hard to blame the company for
its underlying principle of privileging sharing. User autonomy
dictated that individuals should be able to share what they
wanted and the platform should not discourage interactions. As

Zuckerberg and others in the company would put it repeatedly over the coming years, "We do not want to be arbiters of truth ourselves." But nobody would *want* Facebook to arbitrate competing claims about truth.

The question Facebook was asking was evidently the wrong one. The question was not whether Facebook should evaluate and make decisions concerning the veracity of information on the platform. Rather, it was a simple set of questions that required serious research to be applied to all of the platforms: What is the impact of false information on platform users, the broader public, and public institutions? If that impact is appreciable and problematic, what should platform owners do to police this kind of content? What should governments do?

Unfortunately, ask any internet researcher—anyone who studies media or technology and society—and you will hear a familiar story: Facebook doesn't let us evaluate its data. Few researchers believe that Facebook has been friendly to the kind of research that would have identified the risks in its variety of products that allowed for the sharing of information and the trending of news. It was only in the spring of 2018 that Facebook reached agreement with a consortium of researchers led by Stanford University to evaluate the impact of Facebook in the context of elections. At the same time, the press has uncovered stories indicating that Facebook understood well before the Trump election that nefarious actors—particularly Russian troll factories and Russia's Internet Research Agency—were creating and amplifying fake accounts and fake stories in a concentrated disruption campaign targeting the UK, the United States, and later other governments in Europe.

The public had ample reason to be angry. The trick for Facebook was to address this pervasive problem in a way that would empower users to get the truth and not turn Mark Zuckerberg into its arbiter.

Researchers at the Oxford Internet Institute (OII) define online disinformation, or computational propaganda, as "the use of algorithms, automation, and human curation to purposefully distribute misleading information over social media networks." This definition recognizes that the disinformation problems we face depend upon both technology and human agency. OII has shown how all sorts of actors try to manipulate public opinion, from whether to vaccinate your children to whom to vote for in contested elections—governments operating in their own countries and abroad, non-state actors of all kinds, political campaigns and candidates, and others.

In a 2018 study, OII's Samantha Bradshaw and its research director, Philip Howard, noted that, while "understanding precisely how social media platforms impact public life is difficult,"

> ...the absence of human editors in our news feeds also makes it easy for political actors to manipulate social networks.... Social media have gone from being the natural infrastructure for sharing collective grievances and coordinating civic engagement, to being a computational tool for social control, manipulated by canny political consultants, and available to politicians in democracies and dictatorships alike.

OII research has shown not only how foreign and domestic actors abuse the tools of social media to target particular

92   audiences but also how social media platforms present such
      easy marks. They seem designed to be abused, since the same
      tools that generate advertising dollars for them—virality,
      individual targeting of messages, ad placement alongside
      clickworthy videos and stories—also make amplified disin-
      formation so simple.

      Sociologist Zeynep Tufekci has shown how platforms like
      YouTube enable extreme material to find ready audiences. You-
      Tube and Facebook may not *want* to promote marginal, conspir-
      atorial, and extreme content—but there is no denying that they
      make a lot of money from a model that serves up video after
      video, or post after post, that takes one further and further away
      from verifiable information and toward the clickbait world of
      disinformation that intends to meaningfully deceive an audi-
      ence. Their incentives to constrain it are weak.

      OII research has shown that there are steps that the compa-
      nies should and can take without engaging in censorship. Some
      of those steps are technical, treating botnets that amplify disin-
      formation in much the same way companies block spam. Their
      algorithms can be adjusted to prioritize values other than click-
      ability. Just as important, platform owners can deploy greater
      tools of transparency so that users may begin to understand
      the source of material they see on the networks. The companies
      should allow users not only greater insight into the algorithms
      that shape what information they see but also greater control
      over the algorithms that serve up information to them. Most
      cannot achieve the zap-the-bogus-stories hope expressed by
      the *New York Times*.

      Would these steps interfere with company business models?
      Quite possibly, yes—and that should not be an objection. It is

COLUMBIA GLOBAL REPORTS

not very convincing for corporations to complain about such
interference when they are among the most valuable businesses
in the world and have such a strong, often harmful, impact on
public life.

While computational propaganda poses real threats to public
space, the same can be said for regulatory responses. Solutions
to disinformation can easily lead to censorship and constraints
on legitimate content.

    This is not mere theorizing about potential risks of regu-
lation or of the heated rhetoric against "fake news." The trends
have been worrisome since the 2016 election. In 2017, Malaysia
adopted a law that expressly named and criminalized the creation and sharing of fake news. Only through the unexpected
victory of a coalition of opposition groups in the subsequent
national election was it possible to imagine Malaysia repealing
it. Italy adopted a policing mechanism that would allow citizens to report "fake news" to law enforcement. France pursued
restrictions on the sharing of information around the context
of elections, which French officials vigorously defended in the
face of repeated rejections by the French Constitutional Court.
I imagined that many of the leaders in these countries and elsewhere shared the perspective of the *New York Times* about zap-
ping fake stories with fancy algorithms. I feared that they would
take that over-optimistic position about the power of technology to put pressure on companies to scrub their platforms,
a process that, if done ham-handedly, would undoubtedly lead
the companies to restrict a vast amount of troubling, provocative, racy, objectionable content that is nonetheless safe—as a
matter of law—from the reach of government restrictions.

94   Online propaganda is as new as online space, and the energy around addressing it was dominated early on by the fix-it-now-fix-it-fast front. It was not entirely clear if international norms spoke to how governments should address it. With that in mind, two collaborators and friends of mine, Dunja Mijatovic and Edison Lanza, and I made common cause to create that framework. Mijatovic had been a broadcast regulator in Bosnia before the Vienna-based Organization for Security and Cooperation in Europe (OSCE) appointed her in 2010 as its chief monitor of freedom of the media for all of the OSCE's fifty-seven member states. She was widely seen as a no-nonsense voice for press freedom in Europe, respected for standing up to anti-press laws and policies in Europe from Azerbaijan to Russia and Turkey, and to the mass surveillance conducted by the UK, France, and United States. Edison Lanza grew up in Uruguay when it was run by military dictatorship, and he became a reporter, lawyer, and activist, appointed by the Inter-American Commission for Human Rights as its "special rapporteur" for freedom of expression. Not every region of the world has a free speech monitor, but Europe and the Americas do, and since I held a portfolio with a global mandate from the UN, Mijatovic, Lanza, and I work closely together to combat threats to free expression.

Dunja, Edison, and I shared the belief that online disinformation had become a legitimate global concern and that the public and governments would be pushing companies to deal with it. But we also shared the view that steps against disinformation would be tricky, a potentially disruptive force for free expression. After all, human rights law guarantees everyone's right to "seek, receive and impart information and ideas of all kinds." It allows for restrictions that are provided by law and necessary and proportionate to protect vital interests such as the rights of others (e.g., privacy) or national security and public order. But human rights law does not include an exception enabling restrictions merely because the information or ideas are "false." We were worried that a rush to prohibit "fake news," rather than finding a combination of technical, educational, and legal solutions, would almost certainly undermine the protections for free expression over the long term. We wanted to caution governments and companies against taking precipitous steps that could undermine debate and dissent. An emerging hysteria made us worry that democratic states might move so quickly that they would not pay adequate attention to the risks of speech regulation or the implications of making demands on companies that they act as arbiters of truth on their platforms.

There was no specific legal framework apart from several human rights treaties and interpretations by courts and other monitoring bodies, so we decided to create one ourselves. It had become a tradition that we—or our predecessors, along with our colleagues from the African human rights system—would issue an annual statement laying out legal principles that, in our view, governed a particular threat to free expression. We worked with Pansy Tlakula, our counterpart in the African Commission for Human and Peoples' Rights, and two outside organizations, the Halifax-based Center for Law and Democracy and Article 19, to develop a kind of soft law framework to deal with disinformation.

On March 3, 2017, we met in Vienna to issue a "Joint Declaration on 'Fake News,' Disinformation, and Propaganda." The Joint Declaration recognized the legitimate concern that online disinformation could itself be a free expression problem, by

96   misleading populations, drowning out verifiable information, and making it harder for individuals to distinguish fact from fiction. It implicitly acknowledged that governments and the private sector would have to take steps to address the problem.

But we were not at all sanguine that governments would do the right thing. Trump had already coopted the phrase "fake news" as a cudgel to use against critical media—and had already started his insidious descriptions of the media as "enemy of the people." Others around the world followed his lead. The Joint Declaration had to be designed to resist the broad attacks of Trump, who was also developing his own personal and administration-wide program of disseminating propaganda.

We made three main points: First, under human rights law, a government cannot censor expression merely because of its falsity. Any government that wants to restrict disinformation would have to abide by well-established legal principles. Any regulations should be narrowly tailored to solve a particular problem, not a tool that, purposely or not, sweeps in lawful expression.

Second, governments and their leaders have a duty to avoid making or disseminating disinformation and propaganda. The fight against disinformation starts with politicians speaking truthfully. They should be promoting a free and independent media, not undermining it.

And third, we urged platforms to be transparent about their rules and to support technical solutions to disinformation that would strengthen user autonomy and individual ability to separate fact from fiction. The Joint Declaration gave support to fact-checking services and to company review of their advertising models as facilitators of disinformation.

The Joint Declaration set out principles that, in our view, could guide government and company responses to disinformation. It has been picked up and cited around the world, but its overarching message—fighting disinformation begins with *governments* telling the truth—has gone unheeded by far too many in positions of power.

Nearly two years after Trump's election, the *Times* published another editorial that reflected how the paper had matured in its thinking about disinformation. Gone was the call for Facebook to zap fake news items and remove them from the platform. The *Times* claimed that Facebook was relying too heavily on journalists and others in civil society to report instances of disinformation. The company itself, the paper argued, should be developing the tools to remedy this particular platform ill.

For its part, Facebook took some time to supplement its user-centric approach with greater company action to deal with amplification and automation. At a meeting I organized with Article 19 in February of 2017, a number of experts seemed particularly attracted to what several were calling "signals of authority."

According to this idea, the platform could provide signals to users concerning certain kinds of information. For instance, if you hovered your cursor over a shared news item, you might be able to see the URL where the item originated, the age of the URL, claims against the URL, and other clues that might enable a savvy news consumer to discern underlying problems with the provider of the information. A new URL, for instance, might compare unfavorably to the URL of well-established media sources.

The signals-of-authority approach tracked the thinking of fact-checking organizations that believed it was important

98   to identify disputed and debunked stories. It's a powerful tool, but even fact-checkers will explain that debunking and flagging are part of a broader problem. Indeed, some research has suggested that flagging an item as false may have relatively little impact on the reader's belief in the truth of the story. If that is true, fact-checking and other signals would need to be supplemented with attacks not only on specific stories but the particular *virality* of disinformation.

Facebook employees, in my experience, seem committed to checking the amplification of disinformation. They have been building relationships with fact-checking organizations. After nearly eighteen months of struggle to come up with policy, the Facebook news blog posted an announcement of the company's strategy to combat disinformation: a three-pronged approach comprised of enforcement of Community Standards such as the policy against impersonation and the real names requirement; ameliorating the spread of false information without taking it down, using fact-checkers and bot-detection technology; and providing tools to deliver more context around posts. The preference for non-deletion is smart, as it enables the company to avoid the arbiter-of-truth problem. But experts remained uncertain—even two years after Trump's election—as to what Facebook's main efforts against disinformation involved. Whether it's a problem of public relations and transparency or something deeper, there is not a lot of confidence that any of the companies have a handle on how to deal with the flood of propaganda and lies that have spilled onto their platforms—and that their algorithms seem ready to push to users.

The Challenge of the "Partly Free"

By the spring of 2017, voters in the United Kingdom had chosen to take the UK out of the European Union in a Brexit referendum tainted by legitimate charges of disinformation and propaganda. France and Germany were both about to conduct national elections amidst claims of Russian efforts to interfere through disinformation. Spain was contending with an energized independence movement in Catalonia, one that European sources claimed was marred by significant Russian disinformation. The president of the European Commission, Jean-Claude Juncker, called it "one of the most testing periods" in EU history.

Anxiety over disinformation threatened to lead the European Commission to take steps that could undermine independent media more broadly. One Commissioner spoke about "the weaponization of on-line fake news," which, he said, "requires a clear-eyed response based on increased transparency, traceability and accountability." This meant undermining the anonymity that is often critical for public debate and, in the wrong hands, could lead to real repression of activists and journalists.

In 2018, the Commission appointed a "High Level Experts Group," hoping for cover for some of the most far-reaching ideas, but the experts instead issued a reasoned call for study and caution: research before regulation, educational rather than punitive steps, transparency and autonomy. Still, an official communication on online disinformation that April should have rattled the companies:

> These platforms have so far failed to act proportionately, falling short of the challenge posed by disinformation and the manipulative use of platforms' infrastructures. Some have taken limited initiatives to redress the spread of online disinformation, but only in a small number of countries and leaving out many users. Furthermore, there are serious doubts whether platforms are sufficiently protecting their users against unauthorised use of the personal data by third parties.

The implication is that if corporations do not act substantially to address disinformation, regulation will follow. But the Commission fears, more than anything else, fragmentation—that is, each member state making its own laws regulating online speech. They already see that happening with disinformation proposals in Italy, France, and the UK, and the example of NetzDG in Germany provides a template of real concern. Action combating disinformation has become a tool wielded against government critics in places like Hungary and Poland.

So far, the Commission has opted for a soft approach not all that different from its early efforts against hate speech. They decided to pressure the industry, as one participant in the Commission's outside expert group put it to me, to "jointly articulate publicly what they will do and be held accountable on, and

then be judged by the court of public opinion and over time regulators who judge whether it's sufficient." Under Commission
pressure, the companies adopted a Code of Practice to curtail
ad placements alongside disinformation and promote disclosures of political ads, technical responses to the misuse of bots,
empowerment of users to distinguish verifiable facts from disinformation, and enabling research access to the companies.

Some look at the Commission's work and see it as tepid,
lacking powerful incentives for the companies to fix the fake
news problem. Others may suggest we look elsewhere, not at
specific "fake news" legislation but privacy law. Karen Kornbluh of the Council on Foreign Relations argues that Europe's
new and much-heralded digital privacy regulations that entered
into force in 2018, the GDPR, may undermine the ability of "bad
actors" to "tailor disinformation" because "they will have less
access to personal data than they once did." Yet even so, the
rhetoric of European demands is already having a global impact.
In places where independent journalism struggles to survive
against government pressure, high-level European and American hysteria are feeding into the potential for new rules that
could undermine a free press.

Regimes that are either non-democratic or tend to resist democratic ideals, like a free press, often outright criminalize the
dissemination of false information. The laws on disseminating false information in authoritarian regimes are only inci-
dentally concerned with the kind of disinformation that has
overtaken public debate. Many of the governments that criminalize it are themselves its leading practitioners. There is
a great potential for any rules that deal with the content of

expression—particularly whether it is true—to be used for illegitimate purposes even when there may also be a valid reason for those rules.

Singapore, an economic dynamo of a city-state with 5.5 million people, has a well-known distaste for dissent and graffiti, but does not have any evident problems with disinformation. Singapore did not face an election subverted by fake news. It did not have to deal with online incitement to harm refugees. Still, making reference to the debate in Europe and North America, the government asserted, "Singapore should not wait for an incident to occur."

The Singaporean Parliament's Select Committee on Deliberate Online Falsehoods conducted eight full-day hearings into the issue, inviting journalists, academics, and industry representatives who supported non-regulatory approaches. Kirsten Han was one of those journalists, a freelancer with bylines around the world and the editor-in-chief of the Singaporean online outlet New Naratif. She had become known in Singapore and abroad as a strong journalistic voice for human rights and free expression.

Han's written testimony concluded that legislation against "deliberate online falsehoods" or "fake news" would necessarily be overbroad. She argued that it would be subject to abuse and that Singapore instead needed media literacy programming and openness from public institutions to build social "resilience" against disinformation. Something in the testimony captured the attention of member of Parliament Edwin Tong, a member of the committee who inadvertently showed just how dangerous the criminalization of disinformation could be.

Tong homed in on one point: Han had written that, while the Singaporean Constitution guarantees freedom of expression,

Reporters Without Borders ranked the country 151 out of 180 countries in terms of press freedom. Freedom House described Singapore as only "partly free," and Human Rights Watch "details the many ways in which freedom of expression has been restricted in the country." HRW had released a report the previous December focusing on the suppression of free expression in Singapore. The government hated it. In fact, in its own testimony before the committee, the think tank of the ruling People's Action Party submitted a paper that focused on the HRW report as an example of the kind of disinformation that had to be regulated. Han had referred to the report, among others, to reinforce her pre-existing view that Singapore already had ample laws that addressed disinformation. Tong evidently did not like the reference. I am paraphrasing a long exchange that went like this:

Tong: In the Human Rights Watch report, you are one of the thirty-four people interviewed, yes?

Kirsten Han: Why is that relevant?

Tong: You rely on the report for your conclusions. You use it as a platform to make the point that restrictions of disinformation should be understood in this context.

Han: No, I rely on a lot of other sources. And my own opinion is that restrictions are excessive.

Tong: You raised the report, so it is fair for me to ask. Were you one of these thirty-four?

Han: Why is this relevant?

Committee Chairman: You need to answer the question.

Han: Yes, I was one of the thirty-four.

Tong: Would you agree that thirty-four is a small sample?

Han: Yes, but they were of particular experience. They were in practice, observers, etc.

Tong: It would be easy to find thirty-four people . . . thirty-four out of a country this size would be a very small sample.

Han: Well, yes.

MP Tong then tried to pick apart cases in the Human Rights Watch report that he believed to be disinformation. For instance, he noted one case concerning an opponent of capital punishment who wrote about the judiciary's treatment of the issue. His criticism led the government to prosecute him on the basis of Singapore's prohibition of *scandalizing the judiciary*. Human Rights Watch discussed the case as a restriction on expression based on how it constrained criticizing judicial opinions. Tong suggested that HRW falsely claimed that the critic was sent to prison for opposing the death penalty—but HRW did not say that, as Han pointed out. Regardless, it is *this* dispute—the interpretation of HRW's views—that is so revealing, since Tong regards the report itself as a piece of disinformation that evidently could be subject to restriction.

In September, the committee released its report. In some respects, it reflected Han's calls for Singapore to ensure education in critical thinking skills and other non-regulatory approaches to resist disinformation in the future. But it also recommended the criminalization of deliberate online falsehoods. And that is exactly what Han and others feared. A government

that criminalizes disinformation, Han testified, is likely to use
the power broadly, undermining all sorts of expression that fails
the standards of human rights law and punishing or deterring
criticism and robust disagreement.

A repressive approach, one that involves criminalization of
harms that are difficult to identify and easy to abuse, is a natural
takeaway for governments lacking a tradition of tolerance for
dissent and free expression.

Kenya presents a different kind of cautionary story. Democratic
and "partly free," according to Freedom House, Kenya adopted a
law in 2018 designed in part to address the perceived threat of
"fake news." But its approach does more to highlight the abuse of
regulation, particularly in the hands of politicians familiar with
using disinformation as a tool against opponents. I called Mercy
Mutemi, the lawyer for the Nairobi-based Bloggers Association of Kenya ("BAKE"), to understand the environment and the
effort in Kenya. When I reached her on Skype, she began not
with the law but with bullets and tear gas canisters. She wanted
me to understand the complicated background behind Kenya's
recent efforts to deal with disinformation.

President Uhuru Kenyatta was facing opposition leader
Raila Odinga in 2017. On election day, August 8, fabricated stories on social media claimed that Kenyatta had won, even before
polls had closed, and problems of transparency and reporting
by the electoral commission raised tensions. Odinga called the
elections a fraud, and though he asked his supporters for calm,
people took to the streets. (Later, when the Supreme Court of
Kenya ordered new elections because of procedural irregulari-
ties, Odinga and his NASA Party boycotted them.)

In Nairobi's Kibera neighborhood, many of whose residents live in extreme poverty, Mutemi could hear rising protests and the efforts of riot police to tamp them down. As the protests increased in size and intensity, and Mutemi heard the unrest herself, @kot ("Kenyans on Twitter") began to tweet and retweet images of the unrest. Kibera was a danger zone and @kot wanted people to know what was happening. But the security services and police were not pleased. They claimed the images and videos were faked and demanded they be removed. Mutemi called it "the fake newsing of real news." Anything shocking or controversial gets labeled "fake news," regardless of its veracity.

"We have been running on fake news and propaganda all my life, on controlled truth," Mutemi told me. Kenya's blogging culture is vibrant, edgy, often newsworthy and reportorial, occasionally wrong and a subject of controversy in a country that has politics coursing through its public veins. Blogging is both an antidote to and an element of that environment.

By the time of the August 2017 election, "everyone was talking about fake news," Mutemi tells me, a comment echoed by others I've spoken with in Kenya. The U.S. Embassy in Nairobi launched a program to educate voters about the need to distinguish verifiable from fabricated news, to be good media consumers. The European Union's election monitors for Kenya, reporting soon after the poll, explained:

> A high number of well-produced false news items distributed on social media, reportedly in part by political camps, attempted to delegitimise genuine stories about political rivals.... Social media provided important platforms for the

exchange of information about the elections, but also appeared
to reinforce inflammatory messages during the campaign.

In a country where politics tends to dominate the national conversation, one study found that "90 percent of people suspected having seen or heard false/inaccurate information regarding the election." Most of the information was seen or heard online, particularly the widely used WhatsApp messaging service owned by Facebook.

While allegations of fake news trigger concerns in Europe and the United States about the integrity of elections, Kenyans have reasons beyond that to be concerned. In late 2007, almost immediately after authorities had announced the reelection of Mwai Kibaki as president, inter-ethnic violence left nearly 1,200 people dead and approximately 350,000 people internally displaced. Kenya's power struggles had long settled upon regional and ethnic divisions, but violence at this scale was rare in the decades since the country gained independence. The Kenyan media, with its supply of diverse views across the political and social spectrum, had become an important aspect of Kenyan public life. And yet, as the country's Human Rights Commission put it in its post-election violence report in 2008, some elements of the media had allowed politicians at the national and local level to disseminate hatred and disinformation, without much in the way of challenge.

The 2013 elections passed relatively peacefully, but against the historical background of the 2007–2008 violence, and the increased presence of social media and messaging applications like WhatsApp, many Kenyans feared what would happen during the elections of 2017. Social media had reintroduced the

108 possibility of violence. At the same time, the Kenyatta government was showing itself to be remarkably thin-skinned when it
came to criticism and political attack. It put increasingly intense
pressure on the media and non-governmental organizations
critical of its policies. A joint report by Article 19 and Human
Rights Watch detailed the ways in which the Kenyatta administration intimidated journalists. The government had begun
to use Article 29 of the Kenya Information and Communication Act, which criminalizes any person who "sends a message
that he knows to be false for the purpose of causing annoyance,
inconvenience, or needless anxiety to another person."

Shortly before the August elections, the administration
copied the European model of addressing free expression concerns by focusing on the medium rather than the speaker, and
by outsourcing speech regulation to internet companies. Government authorities issued joint guidelines to counter "undesirable bulk political SMS and social media content." The
guidelines were broadly worded, applying to "political messages" deemed "offensive, abusive, insulting, misleading, con-
fusing, obscene, or profane." They provided that social media
content must use "language that avoids a tone and words that
constitute hate speech, ethnic contempt, and incitement."
BAKE called the guidelines "blatantly unconstitutional." All
sorts of content providers would be expected to block violating
messages within forty-eight hours.

After the elections, the government went further. President Kenyatta signed into law the Computer Misuse and Cyber-
crimes Act, which threatened fines and prison for anyone who
"intentionally publishes false, misleading, or fictitious data
or misinforms with intent that the data shall be considered or

acted upon as authentic." BAKE challenged the law in Kenya's Constitutional Court, arguing that the false news provisions would chill expression, undermine the ability of the media to hold government officials accountable, and detract from journalists' capacity to earn a living. The court found BAKE's arguments compelling and issued an injunction against the law's enforcement pending a fuller review and hearing.

Mercy Mutemi, BAKE's lawyer, sees the Computer Misuse Act as a cynical attempt by politicians to protect their reputations and hide corruption.

"Let me surprise you," she said to me. "All the big pronouncements that 'fake news is bad for society'? When the bill was being discussed in Parliament, not even one public interest reason was put forward. One legislator said his marriage was threatened by news of an affair. Another claimed that young people are idle and have nothing to do with their time, so they spread fake news. When you really interrogate it, there is simply no public interest issue behind the law. And indeed, ever since the election period, the mention of fake news has really gone down."

"We got it right with the diagnosis of the problem in 2008," she continued. "Ethnic hatred was at the root of the violence. There was an impression at that time that the internet was something you could control. The internet was seen as a bad thing. The Constitution does not protect propaganda for war, hate speech, or incitement to violence. But fake news? Let's call it lies. Lies are speech and speech is protected. Freedom of expression extends to the freedom to lie, and if your expression doesn't fall into one of those unprotected categories in the Constitution, there's no basis to control it (outside civil defamation)."

Mutemi thinks efforts to clamp down and shrink the space for public opinion on the internet cut against the trends in Kenya, but they do reflect trends elsewhere in East Africa. "Leaders in Uganda and Tanzania behave like they are benevolent dictatorships. But we have all come to value dearly freedom of expression. In Kenya, the blogging atmosphere has become very popular over the last five years. Social media, especially WhatsApp, lets even old people talk about politics. That's how we know everything, how even poor people get relief food. And people feel, 'We can finally speak! We can finally say what we think!'"

"So," Mutemi added, "when you see the language in the law prohibiting a person from 'publishing,' we all wonder what it means. If I forward a message on WhatsApp? If I tweet? If I give my opinion? Suddenly there was panic — 'This is my last tweet; I'm going to be arrested for this' — and people started to see how this could affect them. You had cabinet secretaries threatening to arrest journalists merely because of questions. Now people see the Act as a selfish agenda, a plan to lie to citizens."

Mutemi concluded with a point that I hear often around the world. "With the internet, we don't have the most sophisticated legislators. I had a conversation with a parliamentary committee, and I asked how they would enforce the law when someone 'publishes' anonymously. You have wonderful procedures for warrants, I told them, but how are you going to find that person? And, on our end, it was not like we would propose a way forward."

Kenyans across the political spectrum may be concerned that false claims could contribute to ethnic violence. Recent

history would support that sensitivity. And yet their government adopted a law that seems instead to serve as a protective
shield for politicians and their reputations. It was simply a legal
tool to deter criticism, protest, uncomfortable questions, and
investigative reporting.

Conclusion

Policing Speech
in a Centralizing Internet

Today, a few private companies, driven to expand shareholder value, control social media. And yet the rules of speech for public space, in theory, should be made by relevant political communities, not private companies that lack democratic accountability and oversight. If left alone, the companies will gain ever greater power over expression in the public sphere. While there may appear to be a benign quality to this governance, particularly within the trenches of the new private bureaucracy of content moderation, the companies cannot be expected to be public interest—minded governors and adjudicators of speech over the long term. The demands of the market and majority opinion will inexorably lead to avoidance of controversy and overindulgent respect for public authorities and their power, risking especially the kind of expression that is essential to open political systems.

Governments see that company power and are jealous of it, as they should be. Emmanuel Macron said directly when he appeared before the UN's Internet Governance Forum in November 2018 in Paris: "I deeply believe that it is necessary

to regulate." Macron is not alone. Other democratic govern-   113
ments are also making explicit demands that social media companies regulate their platforms in accordance with national laws
or assertions of public security. Europe has been in the lead,
pressed forward by France, the UK, and Germany. The European
push for regulation of content has not created tools for democratic control as much as it has asked the companies to establish their own private and unaccountable structures. Europe
says, "These are our rules that we want you to enforce," and then
leaves regulation to these corporate actors.

Authoritarian governments are taking cues from the loose
regulatory talk among democracies. They are doing what they
have long wanted to do—taking control of online expressive
space from corporations and punishing individuals for criticism and reporting. Most authoritarian regimes will do what
they want to restrain online speech, but there is a serious risk
that states in what we might think of as Freedom House's "partly
free" category—transitional ones that see-saw between openness and control, that could tip into blossoming democracy or
creeping authoritarianism—will borrow Macron's language of
regulation and deploy it to constrain debate and dissent. Rebecca
MacKinnon, one of the leading thinkers and activists of the digital age, has warned that internet freedom is threatened not only
by authoritarians "but also by Western companies and demo-
cratically elected politicians who do not understand the global
impact of their actions." Activists and individual users struggle
to have a voice in what has largely been a behind-the-scenes
effort to define the rules for online expression.

Indeed, often forgotten are the users, the individuals
who have grown to rely on social media for communication,

114   commerce, and access to information of all kinds. A recent interaction brought this home to me. After a work trip to Bangkok,
where I met with activists from across South and Southeast
Asia, my family and I took a few days to visit Angkor Wat, the
stunning complex of ancient Khmer temples in Cambodia. We
hired a forty-ish Cambodian man, whom I will call S, to drive us
from the heavily touristed central sites to Beng Melea, an aban-
doned Angkor-period temple about an hour away that jungle
has consumed.

We were lucky that S spoke some English. He wasn't gre-
garious but, as we headed to the Cambodian Landmine Museum
not far away, he shared with us his story of surviving the Khmer
Rouge. He began with the genocide and his family's experience
and ended with contemporary Cambodia, whose government
has become increasingly authoritarian and repressive of speech,
media, protest, and opposition politics. We hadn't prompted a
discussion of politics, but S went there as we passed countless
posters of the prime minister, Hun Sen, telling us that every-
body he knew wanted a different government. We wanted to
know: In a country like Cambodia, where the media face intense
restrictions and online protest can result in detention, prosecu-
tion, and harassment, how did he know this? How did he get his
information?

"Facebook," he responded instantly. Facebook, he told us, is
where people learn things, where they share information. Some
of it is rumor, some from neighbors and friends, and some of it
is reporting people get from the outside world about Cambodia.
It has become, he said, the alternative to state media. Without
it, he was not sure what sources he would have.

The platforms have facilitated ethnic cleansing and racist attacks against the Rohingya in Myanmar. They have permitted disinformation, even in Cambodia where there are allegations that Hun Sen manufactured his popularity on the platform. Yet Facebook in Cambodia also offers an outlet for those who desperately want to know the truth about public authorities. It's a reality that should, at least in part, shape ideas about how to promote human rights and democratic values online.

So to bring back the question from the outset: Who is in charge? What are the tools available to ensure that online speech benefits from democratic control, promoting and protecting freedom of expression, privacy of communications, rights of association and assembly, and other values of free societies? This is not an easy agenda to satisfy.

One possibility: #DeleteFacebook. That may be compelling and relatively pain-free in developed and democratic environments, where the public has access to multiple sources of information and deactivating one's social media account may be a reasonable response to the companies' extractive approach to personal data. It may be healthy for all sorts of other reasons. But for people like S, leaving the platform may not be all that attractive. And because the platforms will continue to have massive influence on public space and norms for the foreseeable future, deactivation does not respond to the specific concerns this book identifies.

Another: Do nothing. Let the market self-regulate, hoping that alternative models of speech regulation can battle for market share. This was the initial model, but it is hardly discussed

116 today, and for good reason: The companies are super-dominant and ravenous, knocking down any future competition (as their purchases of smaller competitors have shown).

The moment calls for a serious rethink, an approach not simply to the rules governing online speech but to the public's participation in making, interpreting and enforcing them. It requires action by the companies, governments and civil society to protect speech in the digital age, not merely incremental changes at the margins of social media's management of the public square. We need new models of content moderation and public oversight, supported and promoted by rights-protecting government regulation, and with a long-term vision of public investment to sustain the infrastructure of freedom of expression in a social media age.

Tarleton Gillespie urges that "the discussion about content moderation needs to shift, away from a focus on the harms users face and the missteps platforms sometimes make in response, to a more expansive examination of the responsibilities of platforms, that moves beyond their legal liability to consider their greater obligations to the public." I agree with that, and I agree with Gillespie's calls for transparency, user agency, and stronger diversity, among other ideas that he argues the platforms should implement. Regardless of how governments decide to regulate the platforms, the companies will need to reform the way they police speech. That reform will require the companies to change the way they operate—the foundational rules they adopt to moderate user-generated content; the oversight and accountability to which they subject their decisions; and the roles that they offer to their users worldwide to ensure that their space

democratizes and benefits users and the public wherever they
operate. The following ideas sketch out the kinds of changes
that would help companies and governments meet the challenges of policing content:

Decentralized decision-making: The companies are not
built to moderate content at global scale. They often alienate
and flatten the cultures across the markets where they operate.
Their algorithmic decisions fit complicated modes of thought
and ideas into quantitative analytics. The content rules allow
extremely limited participation for their users to help create or
enforce them. Jack Balkin, a Yale Law School professor who has
studied speech online and off for decades, once argued about
freedom of expression in the context of digital technologies:

> A democratic culture is democratic in the sense that
> everyone—not just political, economic, or cultural elites—has
> a fair chance to participate in the production of culture, and
> in the development of the ideas and meanings that constitute
> them and the communities and subcommunities to which they
> belong.

The companies, as private stewards of public space, interfere with the idea that their users are engaging in democratic
culture. Users become subjects. In that sense, platform "life"
diminishes democratic culture even as it expands the possibilities of communication.

The companies have not addressed their democratic deficit.
Instead, they have addressed problems of scale by hiring (or
promising to hire) more moderators with language skills and
local or regional political knowledge. This is tinkering, and
while important, far from enough. Local civil society activists

118   and users should have an explicit role in company policymaking. Wherever the companies enjoy a market presence, they should develop multi-stakeholder councils, members of which they would compensate, to help them evaluate the hardest kinds of content problems, to evaluate emerging issues, and to dissent to the highest levels of company leadership. The companies should have "desk officers" in the countries where they operate, people, ideally nationals from that country, who would manage relationships with civil society on a full-time basis. If a presence in-country would subject them to threats, harassment, and intimidation, they could be placed regionally or at headquarters. The companies should also identify particularly vulnerable users based on status (e.g. race, religion, migrant, sexual orientation, gender, etc.) and develop programs aimed at protecting the space for their engagement on the platforms and to protect them against off-platform threats, such as those suffered by Rohingya Muslims in Myanmar or migrants in Germany.

These kinds of programs have risks associated with them. They risk capture by ill-intentioned governments or groups, particularly those that are eager to tamp down opposition to government or promotion of unconventional social or political views. Governments already have the tools to pressure the companies to take action against content that, in their view, violates local law. They should not be given an additional tool to interfere with individual rights at the platform level.

Human rights standards as content moderation norms. Facebook and Twitter both made claims in 2018 that their standards are or should be rooted in the human rights of their users. Richard Allan, the lead executive in Europe, wrote that Facebook looks for "guidance" from human rights law, such as Article 19 of the

International Covenant on Civil and Political Rights, one of the
two central treaties of human rights law. Facebook and Google are
both members of the Global Network Initiative, an effort of activists and companies to ensure that the companies adhere to basic
principles of protection of freedom of expression and privacy.
Jack Dorsey said that Twitter, which has refused to join GNI,
should integrate the values of human rights in its rules. These are
positive steps—but they are hardly even a start.

The companies should make human rights law the explicit
standard underlying their content moderation and write that
into their rules. They are global companies dominating public
forums worldwide. International human rights law provides
everyone with the right to seek, receive, and impart information and ideas of all kinds, regardless of frontiers. It protects
everyone's right to hold opinions without interference. Just
as important, human rights law gives companies a language to
articulate their positions worldwide in ways that respect democratic norms and counter authoritarian demands. It is much
less convincing to say to authoritarians, "We cannot take down
that content because that would be inconsistent with our rules,"
than it is to say, "Taking down that content would be inconsistent with the international human rights our users enjoy and
to which your government is obligated to uphold." It is not a
risk-free answer; governments may ultimately block access to
their platforms. But that itself will cause risks for governments,
given the popularity of the platforms among their citizens and
the authoritarian signal website blocking sends to the world.

Some argue that human rights law applies only to governments and not to companies. But that is rapidly becoming an
archaic way of thinking about the structure of international

120   governance. There is a growing recognition that corporations have responsibilities not to interfere with the rights individuals enjoy, whether it is a multinational company involved in mineral extraction that helps fuel conflict or undermine worker rights, or an internet company sharing user data with an authoritarian regime.

I have also heard it argued that human rights law would permit all sorts of bad behavior that undermines user experience, such as misogynistic harassment and bullying, or that human rights principles would make it more difficult for the companies to address disinformation and, for instance, racism, anti-Semitism, Islamophobia, and homophobia. But while human rights law promotes free expression, it also permits restrictions under certain rule-of-law guidelines. Restrictions must be "provided by law"—or in the context of social media companies, have fixed rules, not subject to their discretion, that are publicly accessible and understandable. Restrictions must be necessary and proportionate to protect the rights or reputations of others, public order or national security, or public health or morals. The companies should explain why they require the adoption or enforcement of certain rules. It means that restricting expression should be the last resort, not the first option, particularly where there may be other tools available to deal with a perceived problem. Under these rules, companies can act to protect all of their users' rights and thus protect against activities that, for instance, seek to silence others' voices, release private information, or use the platforms' tools to incite violence.

Finally, some might say that human rights law is too general for the companies to apply. But companies have ample jurisprudence to draw from, based on court decisions interpreting and

applying human rights law. This jurisprudence can be found in   121
the European Court of Human Rights, the Inter-American Court
for Human Rights, the emerging jurisprudence of regional and
subregional courts in Africa, national courts in democratic societies, treaty bodies that monitor compliance with their norms,
and the work of UN and regional human rights mechanisms.
It is not an answer to say the law does not exist because some
look down upon it as a lesser form of law, or because of ignorance that this body of law even exists.

That said, human rights law alone cannot fix the problems
of corporate dominance. Two other tools are necessary.

Radically better transparency. "Transparency," far from being
a mantra without meaning, is a powerful tool to challenge the
powerful and recover individual agency on the platforms. Particularly in the absence of government regulation and accountability, transparency allows users to decide whether to opt into
the platforms and how to behave on them if they do. Companies
that deal with user-generated content now publish periodic
reports providing aggregate data about government requests for
content and account actions (i.e., takedown of posts, requests
for user data, etc.) and implementation of their own content
rules. They should go further, in at least two ways.

Rulemaking transparency would mean that companies disclose their policy choices and their ever-adaptable content
standards. They should open up their processes and proposals
to public comment and, when they adopt new rules about content, explain clearly how they arrived at the changes. Perhaps
more important is *decisional transparency.* The companies need
to disclose to their users *why* they take certain kinds of content actions—what was the basis of a decision and how the user

122   can appeal it. Clarity into algorithmic decision-making—the inputs into the AI that stands to control expression, not some broadly opaque math—would provide bases for individuals and academics to register serious challenges to company enforcement. Ideally, the companies would establish case law, opening up as much of their decision-making as possible to public scrutiny, while still protecting user privacy. They should be creating public repositories of their decisions, allowing users and the public to evaluate the actual decisions that the companies make.

Industry-wide oversight and accountability. The second tool to maximize the value of human rights norms and local engagement is to subject company rules and decisions to industry-wide oversight and accountability. The companies should work with civil society leaders, activists, and academics to develop what Article 19 has called "social media councils." Facebook has already tiptoed into better appeals processes, as Mark Zuckerberg has started talking about a Supreme Court for Facebook and an external appeals mechanism. Early in 2019, the company released a draft charter for an Oversight Board that could permit appeals to an independent body, with whose decisions Facebook would commit to comply. This seems promising, and Facebook has committed to consult widely as it develops this tool. Across social media, the companies should develop a model of industry self-regulation that involves the careful selection of hard cases, evaluated by experts, assessing whether company decisions are in keeping with human rights norms, and binding on company policy. The companies could develop such oversight on a regional basis, allowing them to be closer to the places where they offer the services of a public square, involving

people from the communities affected by company standards
and enforcement.

Major company rethinking is only one part of the way forward. Government regulation is the other necessary fix. Government regulation should monitor company behavior, protect the space for individual expression, reinforce the need for transparency by the companies and themselves, and invest in the infrastructure necessary for freedom of expression in their countries. In my reporting to the United Nations, I have often focused on what governments should avoid: heavy-handed content regulation; company monitoring of their platforms; filters of content at the point of upload, a practice that would almost certainly over-regulate, or censor, legitimate content; sanctions on the platforms such that they have incentives to take down content but limited incentives to leave up legitimate but "difficult" content; and delegation of decisions about content to the companies without government oversight. Some governments are heading in these unfortunate directions, which will neither promote freedom of expression nor facilitate competition nor even protect users and vulnerable groups.

Those cautions remain important, but there are forward-leaning steps that should be part of the regulation of social media. That regulatory environment should include the following:

Require company disclosures—and legislate government transparency, too. Companies may edge toward better transparency in part because of their fear of government regulation. But even if they start to do so, governments have good reason to demand that the companies disclose their rules and decisions, which would

124   give their public the tools to decide whether to engage on the
platforms, how to do so, and whether to move to other forums
that may be available. Germany's NetzDG has begun to do this,
and the companies have been producing specific reporting
about NetzDG implementation. This is a kind of regulatory
move that could encourage greater public understanding of
platform operation.

But transparency is not a one-way ratchet. Governments
can disclose more about their own demands of companies.
How much user data are they requesting from the companies?
What kinds of legal demands are they making of the companies,
whether through regular legal channels or extralegal ones? How
do they make those requests? Are they based on court orders
or agency discretion? Regular reporting from governments is
essential for people to understand what they need the companies to protect them *from*.

Ensuring a role for public institutions. Governments have been
making regular demands on social media companies to take down
content. In the European context, those efforts have focused on
terrorist content, hate speech, and disinformation. The risk is
that these demands will be made through administrative or law
enforcement bodies, such as the Internet Referral Units, or in less
structured environments, by police or others simply reaching out
to make demands related to content. Such actions undermine the
role of public norms in shaping company behavior. Governments
should instead ensure that any efforts to take down content are
channeled through independent courts or agencies, which themselves are subject to challenge and appeal. This will require significant rethinking about the relationship between a state's
public institutions and the private governance of speech by the

companies. It will especially require thinking creatively about
how governments can retool and specialize their courts so as to
deal with the kinds of subjects arising on the platforms. It is not
credible to ignore the problem. It is counter to norms of democratic control of public forums to outsource such decisions to
private actors.

Support for an environment enabling freedom of expression.
The dominant power of the platforms gives them an outsized
impact on public debate and access to information. Facebook's
role in the massacre of journalism has been well documented. In
light of these threats to democratic control of public space, Tim
Wu makes a compelling case for taking on the monopolistic
power of the platforms with the tools of antitrust, focusing in
particular on how Facebook's ownership of WhatsApp and Instagram undermines competition in social media. Antitrust is
one part of a broader effort to create the conditions for the chal-
lengers to Google or Facebook to reinvigorate the freedom of
expression, independent media, and other public goods.

Governments have other tools, however, and they should
use them. Some long-considered policies should be reinforced. Network neutrality, for instance, helps maintain a foundation for innovators to seek access to audiences, essential for
maintaining the possibility of competition with the dominant
social media platforms. While it is under attack, intermediary
immunity from liability remains an important tool to facilitate
freedom of expression on the platforms. Just as a burdensome
tariff ultimately increases costs for consumers, when governments take steps to limit that immunity, users bear the costs
with greater limitations on expression. This has been the case
in the United States, where 2018's laws aimed at limiting online

126   sex trafficking have led companies like Tumblr to restrict legit-
        imate (i.e., lawful) adult content. Governments should be rein-
        forcing intermediary immunity, not chipping away at it with
        content regulations, and instead using the tools of reporting
        and transparency to give users the ability to decide whether to
        use the platforms.

        Finally, governments need to think forward beyond a reg-
        ulatory model of social media control. They should consider
        investing in models of public service media, modeled on public
        broadcasting, that offer space for communication, debate, infor-
        mation, and promotion of independent media. Governments can
        use the kinds of tools that they often deploy to support inde-
        pendent media abroad—such as foreign assistance programs—
        to support independent media at home.

        Ultimately, we need to answer the question—who is to be
        in charge?—in a way that works for us, as a public and as indi-
        viduals, that enables us to claw back some part of the original
        promise of democratic space the internet originally offered.

Content moderation is a relatively new and exciting field of study. Major book-length treatments have only recently begun to find their way to the public, mostly from American or European/UK publishing houses.

A handful of scholars have gone well beyond others in exploring company content moderation and its impact on society at book length. Sarah Roberts, a professor of information studies at UCLA, has written a pathbreaking series of articles on content moderation—exposing not only the companies' policies but their exploitation of the labor market for moderators—that culminated in her new book, *Behind the Screen: Content Moderation in the Shadows of Social Media* (Yale: 2019). Tarleton Gillespie, a sociologist with appointments at Microsoft Research and Cornell, published a rich exploration of company content moderation policies in his study *Custodians of the Internet: Platforms, Content Moderation, and the Hidden Decisions That Shape Social Media* (Yale: 2018). Nicolas Suzor, a scholar and activist based at Queensland University of Technology in Australia, has just written *Lawless: The Secret Rules That Govern Our Digital Lives* (Cambridge: 2019), which deserves a wide audience for its accessible, policy-oriented approach. A terrific collection of essays is Belli & Zingales, eds., *Platform Regulations: How Platforms are Regulated and How They Regulate Us* (FGV Dereito Rio: 2017). For a comprehensive legally oriented approach to the American platforms, Kate Klonick's 2018 article in the *Harvard Law Review*, "The New Governors: The People, Rules and Processes Governing Online Speech," 131 *Harv. L. Rev* 1598 (2018), provides a detailed examination of how company policies evolved into the kind of bureaucratic governance that I sketch out in Chapters 2 and 3.

Few books or author/activists have influenced my own thinking about the internet and individual rights, and their conflict with authoritarians, as much as Rebecca MacKinnon and her book, *Consent of the Networked: The Worldwide Struggle for Internet Freedom* (Basic: 2012). Zeynep Tufekci, the writer and sociologist at the University of North Carolina, published *Twitter and Tear Gas: The Power and Fragility of Networked Protest* (Yale: 2017), which, like MacKinnon's, explores how digital space has not only expanded the possibilities for communication and public protest but also deepened the ability of governments to repress activists, journalists, and civil society more broadly. Both Mackinnon and Tufekci take us beyond the high-level blandness of policy and into the actual lives lived online and offline by activists and journalists and academics around the world.

The stories in Jack Goldsmith's and Tim Wu's *Who Controls the Internet?* (Oxford: 2008) may seem quaint, but their arguments remain just as relevant today; they were among the first to capture the inevitable struggle that would undermine the utopian vision of the internet as democracy promoter and authoritarian basher. For a detailed and realistic look at Chinese control of internet spaces, I strongly recommend Margaret Roberts, *Censored: Distraction and Diversion Inside China's Great Firewall* (Princeton: 2018). The best (and one of the only) treatments of the Russian internet is Andrei Soldatov and Irina Borogan's *The*

Red Web: The Struggle Between Russia's Digital Dictators and the
New Online Revolutionaries (Public Affairs: 2015).

There is little doubt that the debates of the future will focus on the extent to which Artificial Intelligence tools should be adopted by companies and public authorities. Several studies should be on anyone's reading list. Safiya Noble's *Algorithms of Oppression: How Search Engines Reinforce Racism* (NYU: 2018) should be required reading for anyone who thinks that AI will solve—rather than exacerbate—problems of civil liberties and social inequalities and discrimination. Mark Latonero's *Governing Artificial Intelligence: Upholding Human Rights and Dignity* (Data & Society: 2018), the AI Now Institute's 2018 Report, and the Council of Europe's 2017 study, *Algorithms and Human Rights,* are excellent guides to some of the regulatory issues governments face in addressing AI. Frank Pasquale's *The Black Box Society* (Harvard: 2015) and Cathy O'Neil's *Weapons of Math Destruction* (Crown: 2016) are superb examples of books that teach technology (here, algorithmic decision-making) and entertain (or frighten) at the same time.

I noted in Chapter 6 the work of the Oxford Internet Institute related to disinformation and computational propaganda. There is other exceptional work in the field of disinformation and propaganda. Claire Wardle and Hossein Derakshan published *Information Disorder: Toward an Interdisciplinary Framework for Research and Policy* (Council of Europe: 2017), a worthy companion to the empirical work of OII's Computational Propaganda Project. Yochai Benkler, Robert Faris, and Hal Roberts recently published *Network Propaganda: Manipulation,*

Disinformation, and Radicalization in American Politics (OUP: 2018), a penetrating and deeply disturbing study of the impact of computational propaganda on politics in the United States.

Finally, I will (though I hesitate to do this) end on a self-referential note. In my work for the UN, I have submitted several reports that focus on the issues this book addresses, often in much more detail, addressing many more issues than I do in this book, and always in the context of international human rights law. Those reports—on issues such as encryption and anonymity, content moderation, AI's impacts on human rights, and other topics—may be found collected at the website of the Office of the UN High Commissioner for Human Rights.

In 2014, the UN Human Rights Council appointed me as its special rapporteur on freedom of opinion and expression. Apart from teaching, this has been the most rewarding professional experience of my career, for reasons that begin and end with the remarkable people I have met and worked with in the course of this "mandate." I could not begin to thank everyone. Brilliant people working in the trenches of human rights and internet freedom—some in government and the UN and other international organizations, some in companies, many more in civil society—have introduced me to a world of activism, policy, law, diplomacy, law enforcement, scholarship, and commerce that is shaping the environment for free speech—not just online but everywhere.

I have been truly lucky to have had the opportunity to work on this book with the team at Columbia Global Reports. Nick Lemann not only saw the importance of the subject of online speech early on but he helped shape my approach to the subject and to researching it. Likewise, Jimmy So is a great editor; he challenged me at each point of the reporting and writing to identify the central questions and to convey economically and with maximum force the ideas at the intersection of commercial content moderation and government regulation. Camille McDuffie pulled everything together and brought her deep experience in publishing to make this book happen, along with the design and promotional wizardry of Miranda Sita.

Dalia Dassa Kaye has been and always will be my greatest reader and partner. She allowed me to talk through (over and over) every point, and she read every draft and gave me exactly the right balance of encouragement and critique. Our daughter

132   Danielle read a key chapter, our son Abe consulted at every step, and my sister Sara gave us respite from the demands of Watson the dog.

Several people read parts or all of the manuscript. Very special thanks to Barbora Bukovská, Marcelo Daher, Hossein Derakhshan, Nani Jansen, Joe McNamee, Azin Tadjdini, Amos Toh, Jillian York, and Jeff Wasserstrom. I especially thank Amos, whose engagement on all of the issues in this book (and much more) has helped shape my ideas of contemporary freedom of expression for the past three years, and Marcelo, an unsung hero of many good and important internet things that have come out of the United Nations.

A number of people helped me understand the complicated issues that policing speech online involves. Some are activists in repressive environments whom I cannot mention for risking their safety. Most of the people I identify here spoke to me in the context of this book or in the broader context of the work I do reporting for the UN. I am sure to be excluding many people, but I owe particular thanks to Rasha Abdulla, Kwami Ahiabenu, Chinmayi Arun, Susan Benesch, Irina Borogan, Ian Brown, Cindy Cohn, Peter Cunliffe-Jones, Nighat Dad, Eileen Donahoe, Maryant Fernandez, Dipayan Ghosh, Grace Githaiga, Kirsten Han, Fanny Hidvegi, Tom Hughes, Juliane Hüttl, Dia Kayyali, Daphne Keller, Edison Lanza, Emma Llanso, Raegan MacDonald, Rebecca MacKinnon, Colin Maclay, Katherine Maher, Alexios Mantzarlis, Andre Meister, Peter Micek, Dunja Mijatovic, Mercy Mutemi, Rasmus Kleis Nielson, Suzanne Nossel, Carly Nyst, Danny O'Brien, Faiza Patel, Gill Phillips, Dinah PoKempner, Matthew Prince, Burcu Gültekin Punsmann, Maria Ressa, Augustin Reyna, Sarah Roberts, Michael Samway,

Marietje Schaake, Elena Sherstoboeva, Andrei Soldatov, Brett   133
Solomon, Falk Steiner, Cynthia Wong, Nicole Wong, and Yin
Yadanar.

I wish I could identify the many people at the companies
and in governments who gave me real insight into how they
approach the problems I discuss in the book. I also owe thanks
to Jack Goldsmith and Ben Wittes for inviting me to a Hoover
Institution roundtable, at which I presented my argument about
human rights standards for the companies.

I cannot thank enough my colleague and friend Ramin Pejan
and our students in the International Justice Clinic at UC Irvine
School of Law, many of whom have worked on the issues at the
heart of this book, and my colleagues at the Law School.

It has been a challenging few years for the people who
brought me into this world, and I could never express adequately how much I wish my dad could participate in the conversations that I hope this book will encourage. This is for my
parents, Patty and Jerry Kaye.

NOTES

INTRODUCTION

10 **"spreading propaganda against the Islamic system"**: "Iran Said to Free Imprisoned Pioneer Blogger," Robert Mackey, *New York Times*, November 20, 2014.

11 **"Dear fellow inmates"**: "The Web We Have to Save," Hossein Derakhshan, *Matter*, July 14, 2015.

12 **"nowness"**: "2013: The Year 'the Stream' Crested," Alexis C. Madrigal, *Atlantic*, December 12, 2013.

13 **"manufactured amplification"**: "Information Disorder, Part 1: The Essential Glossary," Claire Wardle, *First Draft*, Jul 9, 2018.

13 *Code: Code and Other Laws of Cyberspace*, Lawrence Lessig (Basic Books, 1999).

16 **gatekeepers of content**: "A History of Online Gatekeeping," Jonathan Zittrain, 19 *Harvard Journal of Law and Technology* 253 (2006).

16 **institutions of governance**: "The New Governors: The People, Rules, and Processes Governing Online Speech" Kate Klonick, 131 *Harvard Law Review* 1598 (2018).

17 **chilled individual expression**: *Digital News Report: Turkey Supplementary Report*, Servet Yanatma, Reuters Institute for the Study of Journalism, 2018.

19 **Zuckerberg told an interviewer**: "Mark Zuckerberg on Facebook's hardest year, and what comes next," Ezra Klein, Vox, April 2, 2018.

19 **Jack Dorsey**: https://twitter .com/jack/status/10279625004388 43397?lang=en

20 **digital rights activists often argue**: https://www.ohchr.org/EN/ Issues/FreedomOpinion/Pages/ ContentRegulation.aspx

22 **"face of the Syrian uprising"**: "How a 13-year-old boy became the face of the Syrian uprising," Harriet Alexander, *Telegraph*, June 5, 2011.

22 **"symbol of Syrian revolution"**: "How a 13-year-old became a symbol of Syrian revolution," Sonia Verma, *Globe and Mail*, June 1, 2011.

22 **Company policy**: YouTube Community Guidelines, May 20, 2011, available on Internet Archive's Wayback Machine.

23 *platform law:* "The Law of the Platform," Orly Lobel, *Minnesota Law Review* (2016), San Diego Legal Studies Paper No. 16-212.

23 **apparently targeted attack**: "Marie Colvin: Syrian regime deliberately targeted journalist, US court rules," Samuel Osborne, *Independent*, February 1, 2019.

CHAPTER ONE

25 **would later disappear**: "YouTube keeps deleting evidence of Syrian chemical weapon attacks," Kate O'Flaherty, *Wired*, June 26, 2018.

136   26   **ten hours of videos were uploaded to YouTube every minute**: Hearing on "Global Internet Freedom: Corporate Responsibility and the Rule of Law," Testimony of Nicole Wong, U.S. Senate Judiciary Committee Subcommittee on Human Rights and the Law, May 20, 2008.

26   **450 hours**: Hearing on "Facebook, Google and Twitter: Examining the Content Filtering Practices of Social Media Giants," Written Testimony of Juniper Downs, House Judiciary Committee, July 17, 2018.

27   **"We don't always get it right"**: ibid

28   **"textbook example of ethnic cleansing"**: "UN human rights chief points to 'textbook example of ethnic cleansing," UN News, September 11, 2017.

28   **"Facebook is the internet"**: United Nations, Report of the Independent Fact-Finding Mission on Myanmar, September 12, 2018.

30   **journalists are imprisoned**: "Myanmar court rejects appeal by jailed Reuters reporters," Thu Thu Aung, Poppy McPherson, Reuters, January 10, 2019.

30   **#DearMark letters**: "#DearMark letters underline that Facebook cares only about the crises it creates in wealthy countries," Hanna Kozlowska, Quartz, May 23, 2018.

30   **commissioned by Facebook**: "An Independent Assessment of the Human Rights Impact of Facebook in Myanmar," Alex Warofka, Facebook Newsroom, November 5, 2018.

31   **digital colonialism**: "Resisting digital colonialism," Internet Health Report 2018, April 2018.

31   **the Indian Government has shut down the internet**: "Mandates of the Special Rapporteur on the promotion and protection of the right to freedom of opinion and expression; and the Special Rapporteur on the situation of human rights defenders," David Kaye and Michel Forst, Office of the High Commissioner for Human Rights, May 9, 2017.

35   **Right to be Forgotten Transparency Report**: "Updating our 'right to be forgotten' Transparency Report," Google's *The Keyword* blog, Michee Smith, February 26, 2018.

35   **Google's own study**: "Three years of the Right to be Forgotten," Bertram et al., Google, 2018.

35   **coalition of NGOs noted**: "Written Observations of Article 19 and Others," *Google Inc v. Commission Nationale De L'informatique Et Des Libertés (Cnil)*, Nov. 29, 2017.

36   **urged the court to adopt strict rules**: "Access to European Court legal submissions clarifies Google Spain case," FP Logue, Dec. 20, 2017.

CHAPTER TWO

39   **notice from Facebook**: "Facebook's program thinks Declaration of Independence is

hate speech," Casey Stinnett, *The Vindicator*, July 2, 2018.

41 **Monika Bickert testimony:** "House Judiciary Committee hearing on Examining the Content Filtering Practices of Social Media," Testimony of Monika Bickert, House Judiciary Committee, July 17, 2018.

42 **Juniper Downs testimony:** "House Judiciary Committee hearing on Examining the Content Filtering Practices of Social Media," Testimony of Juniper Downs, House Judiciary Committee, July 17, 2018.

42 **Nick Pickles testimony:** "House Judiciary Committee hearing on Examining the Content Filtering Practices of Social Media," Testimony of Nick Pickles, House Judiciary Committee, July 17, 2018.

43 **The Twitter Rules:** For an excellent overview of how Twitter's rules developed, see "The History of Twitter's Rules," Sarah Jeong, Motherboard, January 14, 2016.

43 **probing and professional hearing:** Digital, Culture, Media and Sport Committee, February 8, 2018 hearing, UK Parliament.

44 **issued a serious report:** "Disinformation and 'fake news': Interim Report," Digital, Culture, Media and Sport Committee, House of Commons, July 24, 2018.

44 **Mark Warner issued a white paper:** "Potential Policy Proposals for Regulation of Social Media and Technology Firms," Mark Warner, White Paper, 2018.

46 **Kate Klonick:** "The New Governors: The People, Rules, and Processes Governing Online Speech," Kate Klonick, *Harvard Law Review*, March 20, 2017.

47 **Google's Decider:** "Google's Gatekeepers," Jeffrey Rosen, *New York Times Magazine*, November 28, 2008.

48 **"A Honeypot for Assholes":** "'A Honeypot For Assholes': Inside Twitter's 10-Year Failure To Stop Harassment," Charlie Warzel, *BuzzFeed News*, August 11, 2016.

48 **Twitter did not have any rule:** All references to past iterations of platform rules and guidelines may be found at the Internet Archive's Wayback Machine.

50 **increasing specificity:** "Monica Bickert on regulating Facebook," David Talbot and Nikki Bourassa, *Harvard Law Today*, October 23, 2017.

51 **Ranking Digital Rights:** "Content Regulation in the Digital Age," Ilana Ullman, Laura Reed, and Rebecca MacKinnon, Ranking Digital Rights, December 15, 2017.

CHAPTER THREE

53 **early content standards:** "Policing Content in the Quasi-Public Sphere," Jillian C. York, OpenNet Initiative, September 20, 2010.

55 **"cross-checked" pages:** "Working to Keep Facebook Safe," Monika Bickert, Facebook Newsroom., July 17, 2018.

138   55   **Britain First:** "Taking Action Against Britain First," Facebook Newsroom, March 14, 2018.

55   **InfoWars:** "Enforcing Our Community Standards," Facebook Newsroom, August 6, 2018

56   **interview with Channel 4:** Channel 4, *Inside Facebook: Secrets of the Social Network,* first aired July 2018.

56   **The Shadow:** "How an Incendiary Rapper Became a Symbol for Israel's Angry Far Right," Danna Harman, *Haaretz,* May 18, 2016.

57   **published an overview:** "Enforcing Our Community Standards," Facebook, August 6, 2018.

57   **published an overview of in August 2018:** "Working to Keep Facebook Safe," Monika Bickert, Facebook Newsroom, July 17, 2008.

58   *Suddeutsche Zeitung:* "Three months in hell," Burcu Gültekin Punsmann, *Suddeutsche Zeitung,* January 6, 2018.

59   *The Guardian* **newspaper:** "Revealed: Facebook's internal rulebook on sex, terrorism and violence," Nick Hopkins, *The Guardian,* May 21, 2017.

62   **typically known as flagging:** "What is a Flag for? Social Media Reporting Tools and the Vocabulary of Complaint," Kate Crawford and Tarleton Gillespie, *New Media and Society,* July 15, 2014.

63   **human programming and the leveraging of that power:** Report to the UN General Assembly, David Kaye, UN Doc. A/73/348, August 29, 2018.

63   **to negative effect:** "Algorithms of Oppression: How Search Engines Reinforce Racism," Safiya Umoja Noble, New York University Press, 2018.

64   **Mark Zuckerberg has made clear:** "A Blueprint for Content Governance and Enforcement," Mark Zuckerberg, Facebook, November 15, 2018.

CHAPTER FOUR

66   **anti-refugee posts on Facebook:** "Fanning the Flames of Hate: Social Media and Hate Crime," Karsten Müller and Carlo Schwarz, University of Warwick, May 2018.

66   **caught on a hot mic:** "Merkel Confronts Facebook's Zuckerberg Over Policing Hate Posts," Patrick Donahue, Bloomberg, September 26, 2015.

66   **August letter:** a copy of which I have obtained.

67   *Together Against Hate Speech:* "Together against Hate Speech," December 15, 2015.

68   **draft law in hand:** "Combating hate crime and punishable false news: Better law enforcement in social networks," Federal Ministry of Justice and Consumer Protection, March 14, 2017.

71   **the European Commission announced:** "EU Internet Forum:

Bringing together governments, Europol and technology companies to counter terrorist content and hate speech online," December 3, 2015.

72 **Prominent human rights organizations:** "EDRi and Access Now withdraw from EU Commission discussions," Access Now, May 31, 2016.

72 **Article 19:** "EU: European Commissoin's Code of Conduct for Countering Illegal Hate Speech Online and the Framework Decision," Article 19, June 2016.

72 **The Commission responded:** Letter from Věra Jourová to Jens-Henrik Jepperson, June 21, 2016.

74 **"We cannot accept a digital Wild West":** "Security Union: Commission steps up efforts to tackle illegal content online," European Commission Migration and Home Affairs, Sept. 28, 2017.

CHAPTER FIVE

76 **"who claim to be leaders":** R v Darren Osborne, Woolwich Crown Court, Judiciary of England and Wales, February 2, 2018.

77 **adopting broad definitions:** "Mandate of the Special Rapporteur on the promotion and protection of human rights and fundamental freedoms while countering terrorism," Fionnuala Ní Aoláin, July 24, 2018.

77 **limit terrorist content:** Testimony of Sheryl Sandberg, Hearing Before the United States Senate Select Committee on Intelligence, September 5, 2018.

78 **joint British, French, and Italian statement:** "United Nations – Fight against terrorism/cyber security/digital technology/high-level meeting on preventing terrorist use of the Internet – Joint statement by the United Kingdom, France and Italy," Sept. 20, 2017.

78 **"dangerous content":** "PM Speech at UNGA: preventing terrorist use of the internet," September 21, 2017.

78 **"Choose your side":** "Discours du Président de la République - Mission permanente de la France - ONU - Le terrorisme internet," September 21, 2017.

81 **removal of 304,000:** "Counter Terrorism Policing urging public to ACT against online extremism," National Police Chiefs' Council, April 6, 2018.

81 **do not maintain statistics:** FS50722134, Freedom of Information Act 2000, Information Commissioner's Office, June 21, 2018.

81 **"not just lazy, but extremely dangerous":** "Europol's Internet Referral Unit risks harming rights and feeding extremism," Lucie Krahulcova, Access Now, June 17, 2016.

82 **voluntary commitments:** "Proposal for a Regulation of the European Parliament and of the Council on preventing the dissemination of terrorist content

140   online," European Commission, Sept. 12, 2018.

83   **breadth and vagueness are problematic:** "Mandates of the Special Rapporteur on the promotion and protection of the right to freedom of opinion and expression; the Special Rapporteur on the right to privacy and the Special Rapporteur on the promotion and protection of human rights and fundamental freedoms while countering terrorism," David Kaye, Joseph Cannataci, Fionnuala Ní Aoláin, Dec. 7, 2018.

CHAPTER SIX

84   **"liars and con artists":** "Facebook and the Digital Virus Called Fake News," The Editorial Board, *New York Times,* November 19, 2016.

85   **Marietje Schaake:** "Hate speech, populism, and fake news on social media–towards an EU response (debate)," Marietje Schaake, European Parliament, April 5, 2017.

86   **Inspector General of Police:** "Ghana's Inspector General of Police threatens to jam social media on election day," Amandla News, June 17, 2016.

87   **Oxford Internet Institute:** "Challenging Truth and Trust : A Global Inventory of Organized Social Media Manipulation," Samantha Bradshaw and Philip N. Howard, Oxford Internet Institute, July 2018.

88   **"We've been working on this problem for a long time":** https://www.facebook.com/zuck/posts/10103269806149061

90   **consortium of researchers:** "Facebook is Giving Scientists Its Data to Fight," Robbie Gonzalez, *Wired,* May 29, 2018.

92   **Zeynep Tufekci:** "YouTube, the Great Radicalizer," Zeynep Tufekci, *New York Times,* March 10, 2018.

97   **"signals of authority":** "#FakeNews: innocuous or intolerable?", Allen Babajanian and Christine Wendel, University of California Irvine School of Law, April 2017.

98   **experts remained uncertain:** "How Facebook deals with misinformation, in one graphic," Daniel Funke, Poynter, October 25, 2018.

CHAPTER SEVEN

99   **Catalonia:** Catalan independence: EU experts detect rise in pro-Kremlin false claims," Jennifer Rankin, *Guardian,* Nov. 13, 2017.

99   **"one of the most testing periods":** Mission Letter from Jean-Claude Juncker to Commissioner Mariya Gabriel, May 16, 2107.

99   **"the weaponization of on-line fake news":** "EU piles pressure on social media over fake news," Julia Fioretti, Reuters, April 26, 2018.

100   **"High Level Experts Group":** "Next steps against fake news: Commission sets up High-Level

Expert Group and launches public consultation," November 13, 2017.

100 **communication on online disinformation in April 2018:** Communication from the Commission–Tackling online disinformation: a European Approach, April 26, 2018.

101 **Code of Practice:** "EU Code published: another step forward in the right against disinformation," Raegan MacDonald, *Open Policy and Advocacy*, September 26, 2018.

101 **Karen Kornbluh:** Could Europe's New Data Protection Regulation Curb Online Disinformation?" Karen Kornbluh, Council on Foreign Relations, Feb. 20, 2018.

102 **Han's written testimony:** Written Testimony of Kirsten Han, Submission to the Select Committee on Deliberate Online Falsehoods, February 26, 2018.

103 **HRW had released a report:** "'Kill the Chicken to Scare the Monkeys': Suppression of Free Expression and Assembly in Singapore," Human Rights Watch, December 12, 2017.

104 **released its report:** "Report of the Select Committee on Deliberate Online Falsehood," Thirteenth Parliament of Singapore, September 19, 2018.

105 **called the elections a fraud:** "Kenya Election Returns Were Hacked, Opposition Leader Says,"

Kimiko de Freytas-Tamura, *The New York Times*, August 9, 2017.

106 **The European Union's election monitors:** "Democratic commitment demonstrated by the people of Kenya, despite parties' forceful criticism of key institutions," August 10, 2017.

107 **one study found:** "The Reality of Fake News in Kenya," Portland and GeoPoll, July 19, 2017.

108 **intense pressure on the media:** Mandates of the Special Rapporteur on the promotion and protection of the right to freedom of opinion and expression and the Special Rapporteur on the situation of human rights defenders," David Kaye, Michel Forst, Office of the High Commissioner for Human Rights, March 31, 2016.

108 **non-governmental organizations:** Mandates of the Special Rapporteur on the promotion and protection of the right to freedom of opinion and expression; the Special Rapporteur on the rights to freedom of peaceful assembly and of association and the Special Rapporteur on the situation of human rights defenders," David Kaye, Maina Kiai, Michel Forst, Office of the High Commissioner for Human Rights, Feb. 6, 2017.

108 **"blatantly unconstitutional":** "Statement by BAKE on CA's 'Guidelines for Prevention of Dissemination of Undesirable Political Messages,'" James Wamathai, Bloggers Association of Kenya, July 5, 2017.

142   CONCLUSION

112   **"I deeply believe that it is necessary to regulate":** "Discours du Président de la République, Emmanuel Macron lors du forum sur la gouvernance de l'internet à l'UNESCO," *Élysée*, November 13, 2018.

113   **Rebecca MacKinnon:** *Consent of the Networked: The Worldwide Struggle for Internet Freedom* (Basic: 2012), xvii.

115   **Hun Sen manufactured his popularity:** "Opinions Democracy is dying in Cambodia. Facebook should make sure it doesn't help kill it," *Washington Post*, March 4, 2018.

116   **Tarleton Gillespie:** *Custodians of the Internet: Platforms, Content Moderation, and the Hidden Decisions That Shape Social Media* (Yale University Press: 2018), 215.

117   **Jack Balkin:** "Digital Speech And Democratic Culture: A Theory Of Freedom Of Expression For The Information Society," Jack M. Balkin, *New York University Law Review*, Volume 79, April 2004, Number 1.

120   **growing recognition that corporations have responsibilities:** *Guiding Principles on Business and Human Rights: Implementing the United Nations "Protect, Respect and Remedy" Framework*, United Nations, New York and Geneva: 2011.

122   **Oversight Board:** https://newsroom.fb.com/news/2019/01/oversight-board

123   **my reporting to the United Nations:** https://freedex.org/wp-content/blogs.dir/2015/files/2018/05/G1809672.pdf

126   **Tumblr to restrict legitimate adult content:** "Tumblr's Porn Ban Reveals Who Controls What We See Online," Paris Martineau, *Wired*, December, 4, 2018.